THE AMERICAN WEST : MYTH OR REALITY?

In this book we shall be investigating one of the most exciting periods of history. It is also one that has been endlessly retold through books, film and television. Sources 1 and 2 show two classic images of this time: the heroic lawman in a Hollywood film and the violence of Indian attacks painted at the time.

We live in a culture that thrives upon a 'history' made up of fantastic heroes, as the modern historians in Sources 3 and 4 show.

Like all good stories, the critical reader must be aware of possible problems when studying this topic. How much of what we think of as the 'American West' is reality; and how much of it has been changed in our minds by 20th-century writers and Hollywood studios? As you study this topic try to look out for films and TV programmes about the West to compare how closely they match what you learn in this book. Has Hollywood told us the truth?

SOURCE 2

'Attack on an emigrant train', painting by Charles Lidneux.

SOURCE 3

The story of the American West . . . is a heroic world of quests and wars, of journeyings into remote lands, of daring hunts, last stands, and legendary exploits. It is an epic of mighty deeds, of triumphs and failures, of inconsistent heroes and heroines. The West is a tragedy relieved by elements of comedy. It is a tale of good and evil.

Dee Brown, The Westerners, *1974*

SOURCE 4

The western hero in legend is a man of excess. He is a creature of the tall tale . . . He knows no moderation, in gunplay, drinking, or fighting . . . Restless, impatient, he needs no one around him because he is self-sufficient . . . Alone in the wilderness he is supreme.

Robert V. Hine, The American West, *1984*

SOURCE 1

Poster for Wyatt Earp, *starring Kevin Costner, 1994.*

1. Write a list of ten things you associate with the American West.
2. What kinds of problems are there in studying the American West?

3. What impression of the West is being given in Sources 1 and 2?
4. What kind of images of the West have you seen in films and TV programmes?
5. Do you think that historians are more or less likely to be reliable than films and TV?

FINDING OUT ABOUT THE AMERICAN WEST

In some ways it is very easy to find out about the American West as so much has been produced about it. In other ways it is difficult: the last section warned that we must be careful about accepting some evidence as reliable. As you can see in Source 1 we divide sources into two types:

- primary – produced around the time of the event;
- secondary – produced afterwards.

This book is a secondary source, although it is full of written and pictorial primary sources to help illustrate issues. When we use historical sources to help us understand this past we call this **evidence**: it is the skill we have in using evidence appropriately that helps us to make valid points and judgements. Historians need to use both primary and secondary sources. Primary sources allow us to experience the material first hand rather than relying on someone else's interpretation of it: it also allows us to get an empathetic feel for the subject – to gain a better idea of people's beliefs, values and feelings. Secondary sources, such as books, help us to understand the primary sources more, and allow us to see what opinions other historians have had. It is important to see what professional historians have written as they will have done extensive research, perhaps having access to original documents that are not available to us.

SOURCE 1

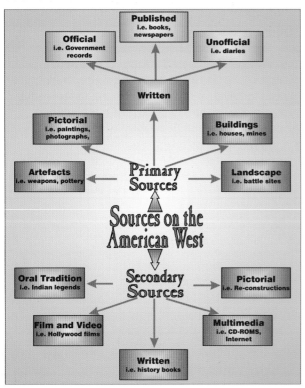

Primary sources on the West need to be handled with care. For example, Source 2 is a description of an Indian written by Francis Parkman in the 1840s.

SOURCE 2

This was an old Kanzas Indian; a man of distinction, if one might judge from his dress. His head was shaved and painted red, and from the tuft of hair remaining on the crown dangled several eagle's feathers, and the tails of two or three rattlesnakes. His cheeks, too, were daubed with vermilion; his ears were adorned with green glass pendants; a collar of grizzly bears' claws surrounded his neck, and several large necklaces of wampum [beads] hung on his breast.

This gives an impressive image. However, a few pages later he writes:

SOURCE 3

A long procession of squalid savages approached our camp. Each was on foot . . . His clothing consisted merely of a scanty cloth, and an old buffalo robe, tattered and filthy, which was hung over his shoulders . . . He carried his bow and arrows in his hand, while his meagre little horse was laden with dried buffalo meat, the produce of his hunting. Such were the first specimens that we met – and very indifferent ones they were – of the genuine savages of the prairie.

Pictorial sources can also cause problems. Source 4 comes from the Hollywood film *Far and Away* (1992) showing people racing to stake claims to land. Is this a reliable reconstruction? Source 5 is a photograph from the period showing a group of black cowboys, very different to most pictures and films which portray cowboys as white. Is this reliable?

The sources in this book are here to allow you to develop your historical skills such as:

- interpretation;
- cause and consequence;
- motivation;
- analysis and evaluation;
- historical judgement;
- comparison;
- similarity and difference;
- change and continuity;
- reliability;
- empathy.

SOURCE 4

From Far and Away, *1992.*

SOURCE 5

Black cowboys, Texas, at turn of century.

However, your best route to success is to question and explain. Another key feature of this book is to help you enjoy this fascinating topic. Enjoy!

1. a) What is the difference between primary and secondary sources?

b) What is evidence?

c) Why is it important to use evidence when studying a topic?

2. Copy out and fill in. Give as many other examples as you can in addition to those in Source 1.

Primary sources

Type	Examples
Pictorial	paintings

Secondary sources

Type	Examples

3. Which are the most reliable: primary or secondary sources?

4. a) Why do you think Sources 2 and 3 are so different?

b) What does this warn us about primary sources?

5. What could you do to check how reliable Sources 4 and 5 are?

5

THE GEOGRAPHY OF THE AMERICAN WEST

We cannot understand the peoples of the American West and the lifestyles they lived unless we understand the natural landscape of the USA and how it affected all aspects of their lives. The scale of the incredible achievement and destruction that took place in the American West makes little sense without knowing about this landscape. However, it is difficult for us to imagine the scale of the area we are studying: Source 1 shows how small the UK is in comparison to the USA. The vastness of the land is matched by the huge contrast in its different environments. Our study focuses on the American West, which begins west of the Mississippi River (see Source 2) and ends on the coast of the Pacific Ocean: from beautifully fertile land, through desert, to snow-capped mountains. It contains some of the most beautiful – and dangerous – landscapes in the world.

In 1840 the Great Plains – now usually called the Prairies – were a huge expanse of wind-swept grassland inhabited by 60 million buffalo and many Indians. In some parts they become semi-desert in the South. Going westward, the Plains give way to the soaring Rocky Mountains, which form a natural barrier that only the bravest or most foolhardy would attempt to cross: there are over 50 peaks over 4,200m high in Colorado alone. Beyond this lies a plateaux region that is semi-desert in many parts, especially in the South. Then there are the Sierra Nevada Mountains rising up to 4,500m. The American West ends with the fertile lands of the Pacific Basin.

SOURCE 1

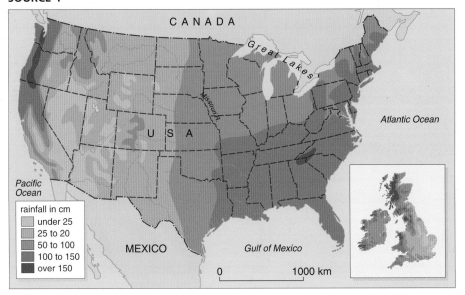

The annual rainfall of the USA.

rainfall in cm
- under 25
- 25 to 20
- 50 to 100
- 100 to 150
- over 150

SOURCE 2

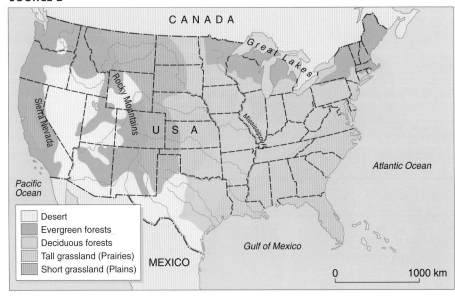

The natural vegetation of the USA in 1840.

- Desert
- Evergreen forests
- Deciduous forests
- Tall grassland (Prairies)
- Short grassland (Plains)

For many people much of this region was known as the 'Great American Desert' (see page 14), and was considered unsuitable for white Americans at the beginning of our period. White Americans also believed in the idea of 'the Frontier' – an invisible dividing line between the land inhabited by white Americans and the 'wilderness' beyond. In 1800 it was drawn along the Appalachian Mountains; and by 1840 it was along the Mississippi River. By 1895 it had gone: the entire West as far as the Pacific Ocean had been colonised by white settlers.

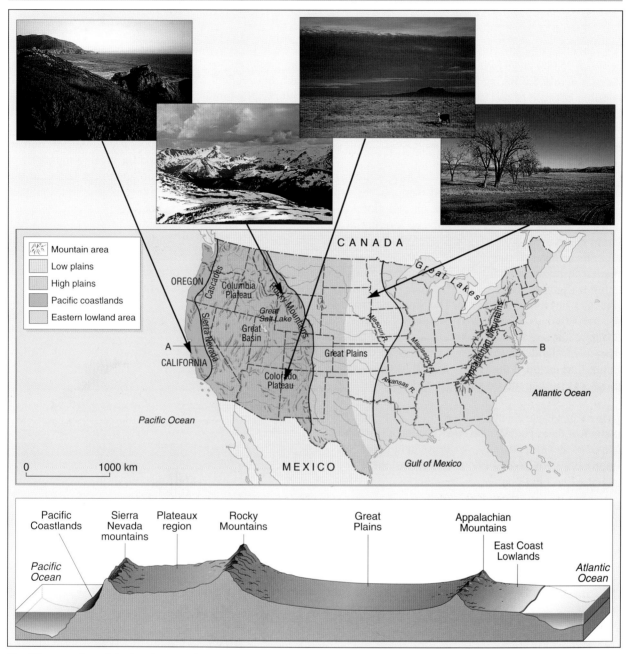

The different regions of the American West in 1840.

1. a) Study Source 1. Which are the wettest and driest parts of the West?

b) How does this compare with the natural vegetation in Source 2?

c) Why do you think some people called this region the Great American Desert?

2. Using Sources 1 to 3 describe the main features of: the Great Plains; the mountains; the plateaux; the Pacific coastlands.

3. Why do you think the West was described as a 'wilderness' in 1840?

4. Why is it impossible to understand the history of this period without studying the landscape and climate?

FINDING OUT ABOUT INDIANS

Ancient Native Americans first arrived on the continent between 25,000 and 35,000 years ago from Asia. Their journey across the Bering Straits (Source 1) was made possible because of an 'ice age' during which the sea level fell, exposing a land 'bridge' linking Asia and America over which people could travel the 72km journey.

Over many centuries these peoples developed lifestyles shaped by the environment around them and by what materials they could use: from shelter and clothing to hunting. In this book we will only be looking at the Great Plains area. Source 2 shows that even within this area there was a wide variety of different Native American peoples, with their own beliefs, values and cultures (Sources 3 and 4). They include famous names like the Cheyenne and Pawnee. The Sioux are probably the most famous. They called themselves a variety of different names, such as Lakota, Nakota and Dakota. They were divided into different tribes, such the Teton Sioux that included the Oglala and Blackfeet: each of these was further sub-divided into bands.

Historians face problems in trying to piece together the history of these peoples. No American peoples north of Mexico developed any written language. Most impressions we have of Plains Indians are the writings of white people who were often hostile towards them and produced very biased accounts. Fortunately, we have an excellent source in the work of George Catlin who travelled among the Plains Indians in the 1830s making hundreds of paintings (Sources 5 and 6). He also produced two volumes of his 'letters' in 1844. Although – like his contemporaries – he referred to them as 'savages', he revealed a great sympathy and affection towards them: 'I look upon the Indian as the most honest and honourable race of people that I have ever lived amongst in my life.'

In this book you will study many aspects of Plains Indians' lifestyles. Many of these are included alongside studies of white settlers' lifestyles to allow you to compare and contrast the two.

SOURCE 2

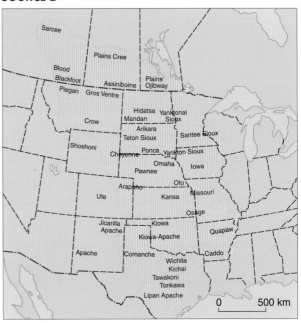

Major peoples of the Plains Indians.

SOURCE 1

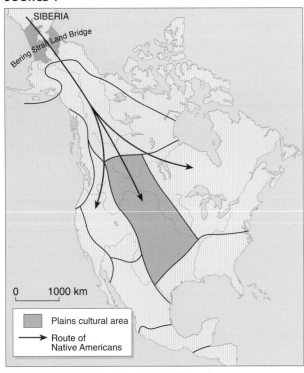

Route of the Native Americans into North America.

SOURCE 3

An Osage chief, by Charles de Saint-Memin, c. 1804.

SOURCE 4

A Mandan chief, by Karl Bodmer, 1834.

George Catlin's painting of a Mandan village showing their lodges made out of locally available materials, 1800. Many Plains Indians preferred to live in portable tipis (see page 46). Catlin's paintings show a large range of different homes and activities.

SOURCE 6

George Catlin's painting of the 'Choctaw Ball Game', 1834–5, which today we call lacrosse. Archery, horse riding, and wrestling were also very popular among men as good training for warfare.

1. How did people first travel to and into America?

2. Copy out and complete using Source 2. For each give three of four examples.

Northern Plains	Central Plains	Southern Plains

3. What problems do historians have in finding out about Plains Indians?

4. What impression is given of the chiefs in Sources 3 and 4?

5. Explain why the work of George Catlin is so important to historians. Use the evidence in Sources 5 and 6 as examples.

Horse and buffalo culture

The horse was one of few good things Europeans gave Native Americans after the Spanish introduced them into North America in the 17th century: there were no horses in America prior to European contact (see Source 7). Although some early Indians were more likely to eat the horse than ride it, its importance soon became obvious.

SOURCE 7

A few times in history, technology has changed so sweepingly and dramatically as to alter a whole way of life. . . . In the Plains during the seventeenth century it was the horse that changed Indian life.

Merwyn S. Garbarino, Native American Heritage, *1979.*

The way of life changed for tribes like the Sioux and Cheyenne. Hitherto they had lived in villages and been unable to travel far onto the Great Plains. Now the 'Big Dog' (as it was often called) transformed their lives. Hunting buffalo on foot had been difficult and dangerous: often they were stampeded over cliff faces. Now most Plains Indians became nomads, that is they were able to travel from place to place. In Source 8 you can see Indians on the move using horses fitted with the travois to drag their belongings: in the past goods were carried by dogs and women. Now Indians followed the great herds of buffalo, fought and raided for horses, and became proud masters of the Great Plains.

SOURCE 8

Sioux Indians moving camp using a travois. Painting by Charles M. Russell.

SOURCE 9

To the Plains Indians . . . the horse meant power and freedom. Up through Apache and Comanche country . . . to the land of the Blackfoot galloped the new way of life . . . Wealth was calculated by the number of horses a man possessed. Instead of a trudging foot-people confined to the fringes of the prairies, the Plains Indians quickly became the finest horse riders in the world. In a sudden blaze of mobility they poured out on to the plains. Farming was forgotten. On horseback they could carry all their belongings easily, and kill more buffalo than they ever dreamed possible.

Kenneth Ulyatt, The Time of the Indian, *1975.*

Horses affected women's lives too. Many men considered their hunting horse more important than their wife: when raiders were nearby some warriors kept their horse in their tipi and made the women sleep outside. The horse also encouraged polygamy – having several wives. With more buffalo being killed by each warrior, more wives were needed to prepare the skins!

The most dramatic use of horses was hunting the 60 million buffalo that roamed the Great Plains, as George Catlin describes in Source 10.

SOURCE 10

The buffalo herds, which graze in almost countless numbers on these beautiful prairies . . . The buffalo is a noble animal, that roams over the vast prairies . . . The buffalo bull is one of the most formidable and frightful looking animals in the world when excited to resistance; his long shaggy mane hangs in great profusion over his neck and shoulders and often extends quite down to the ground . . .

Their flesh . . . furnishes the savages of these vast regions the means of a wholesome and good subsistence, and they live almost exclusively upon it.

George Catlin, 1850.

The hunt was prepared like a religious ceremony with horses and warriors decorated with paint. Each warrior had his own marking on his new iron-tipped arrows so his wives could later identify the animals he had killed. Source 11 is from the film *Dances with Wolves* (1991) and shows a buffalo hunt in progress. Once killed, the women moved in to skin and dismember the beasts.

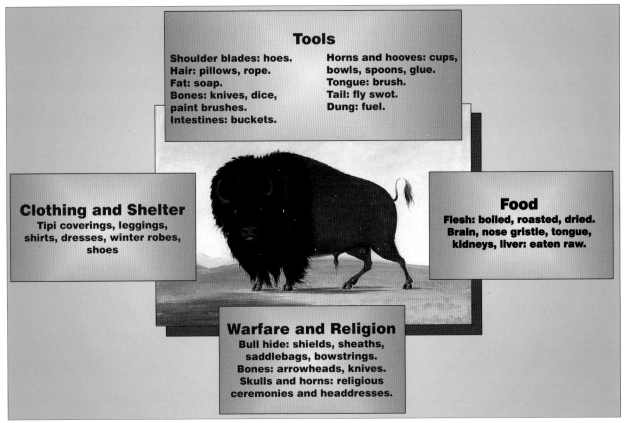

Tools

Shoulder blades: hoes.
Hair: pillows, rope.
Fat: soap.
Bones: knives, dice,
paint brushes.
Intestines: buckets.

Horns and hooves: cups,
bowls, spoons, glue.
Tongue: brush.
Tail: fly swot.
Dung: fuel.

Clothing and Shelter

Tipi coverings, leggings,
shirts, dresses, winter robes,
shoes

Food

Flesh: boiled, roasted, dried.
Brain, nose gristle, tongue,
kidneys, liver: eaten raw.

Warfare and Religion

Bull hide: shields, sheaths,
saddlebags, bowstrings.
Bones: arrowheads, knives.
Skulls and horns: religious
ceremonies and headdresses.

The importance of the buffalo to the Plains Indians.

SOURCE 11

DER MIT DEM WOLF TANZT

Poster for Dances with Wolves, *1991.*

SOURCE 12

The skins were rolled back, with the stench of fresh blood
. . . Then the fine pale tallow and red meat lay clean on the
skins, the visceral parts too, the heads, the great bones for
the marrow . . .

The small intestines were cut into small square pieces, and
with a droplet of bile on each piece, the small children ate
them down like candy.

Mari Sandoz, The Buffalo Hunters, *1954.*

Plains Indians used every part of the beast, as Source
13 shows: the only part left on the Plains was the heart
as they believed that this would ensure the dead animal
was replaced. At one time it looked as if the buffalo
would run forever.

1. When was the 'Big Dog' introduced?
2. Use Source 8 to explain what a travois
   was.
3. How did the horse change the lives of
   Indians?
4. Use Source 11 to explain how the horse was
   used in hunting.
5. Use Sources 10, 12 and 13 to describe the
   importance of the buffalo.

6. Which was most important to the Plains
   Indians, horse or buffalo? Explain your
   answer.
7. 'Plains Indians' lifestyle was dependent
   upon the horse and buffalo.' Explain this
   statement.

SOURCE 14

From Dances with Wolves, *1991.*

Government and warfare

Power rested in the hands of the tribe, divided into bands of 300 to 500. In the summer these bands came together for buffalo hunts and ceremonies. Chiefs had very limited power. Some tribes, such as the Crow and Cheyenne, had councils while others chose leaders for specific events. Source 14 is a reconstruction of a Sioux council meeting from the film *Dances with Wolves* (1991). The Cheyenne had a council of 44 made up of peace chiefs who were considered more important than war chiefs. These were older men chosen to serve for 10 years. They discussed issues such as moving camp, alliances and war. They would also deal with criminals who might be forced to help their victims' families or even banished from the tribe. Most had their own police force in the form of Dog Soldiers to keep the peace in the camp.

Tribal leaders decided about war, the best way for a man to prove himself. This began in adolescence when youths collected items for their medicine bundles to bring them victory in war. Their guardian spirit vision told them what to include in the bundle: often cutting off a finger induced this vision. Indians fought for glory not killing, and would have no hesitation in retreating if the odds were unfavourable. The greatest honour was in getting up close to an enemy, touching him, and retreating safely: this was done with a blunt decorated 'coup' stick: counting coup was important in measuring a warrior's success. Indian warfare could also be brutal against the enemy (see Source 15).

SOURCE 15

Two young men . . . held him fast while he was scalped alive. They then built a great fire, and cutting the tendons of their captive's wrists and feet, threw him in, and held him down with long poles until he was burnt to death.

George Catlin.

Usually scalping took place after death. Scalps were visible signs of a warrior's success in war: scalping was also believed to rob the dead man of his spirit to prevent him entering the afterlife.

---

1. a) What were: bands; councils; Dog Soldiers?

   b) How powerful were chiefs?

2. a) What was the main objective of war?

   b) What was 'counting coup'?

   c) Why did Indians scalp?

---

3. How well suited was Indian government to their lifestyle?

4. In what ways was Indian warfare different to our idea of warfare?

THE SETTLERS

In 1840 the American West was on the verge of a white invasion. Attitudes were changing as more people decided that the western climate could support white settlers, and pioneers carved out the route for them to travel. What happened over the next few decades led to one of the most amazing transformations of a landscape in history.

What types of people ventured west at the beginning of our period? We are lucky to have an account from the time to answer this question.

SOURCE 1

Most of the western population is made up of . . . elements . . . from almost every trade, profession, and position in life. The greatest part is made up of recent emigrants, for the original pioneers of the west are nearly lost in the crowd of newcomers. Substantial householders who have sold out their domains at the east, have here made their clearings and built their comfortable mansions on the soil. However, most emigrants are men of limited means, who have come into this country to improve their standard of living.

. . . They require all the things which belong to a civilised society. To supply this demand, workers in the various trades follow, who are followed by the merchants, and by different professions, who find that the avenues to wealth and distinction in the east are more crowded than in the new country. To these are added settlers, Dutch, Irish, English, Swiss, and immigrants from almost every part of Europe . . . The different elements of society become mixed. Here may be found the ruddy-faced Yankee farmer, with his axe on his shoulder, or the New York merchant . . . Here the English peasant, fresh from the markets of London, mixed with pale-faced Virginians from the banks of the Mississippi . . . The necessary consequence of this state of things is to cause society to appear somewhat crude, rough, and in some ways, even lawless.

The Merchants' Magazine, *1840.*

SOURCE 2

Some of the thousands of emigrants who came from Europe to start a new life.

1. What was most of the population made of?
2. What had the 'substantial householders' done?
3. What types of people were most emigrants?
4. Why did different professions follow them?
5. What was the consequence of 'this state of things'?

6. 'The West was a new, exciting melting pot of peoples.' Does the evidence support this? Explain your answer.

MOVING TO THE GREAT AMERICAN DESERT

Only a few years before the mass influx of people to the West, the area had been generally regarded as totally unsuitable for anyone but Indians. Source 1 gives two typical viewpoints.

SOURCE 1

A) I do not hesitate in giving the opinion, that it is almost wholly unfit for cultivation, and of course, uninhabitable by a people depending upon agriculture for their subsistence.

Major Stephen H. Long, 1820.

B) Undulating and treeless plains, and desolate sandy wastes, wearisome to the eye from their extent and monotony.

Washington Irving, 1836.

This 'desert' made up some 30% of the country, divided into three strips:

- east – high plains;
- centre – mountains;
- west – inter-mountain area and the Great Basin.

The altitude ranges from 81m below sea level in Death Valley to over 4,200m in the mountains. Temperatures range from –20˚C in the winter to 65˚C in the summer. Even today these statistics are daunting for most people. So why did so many people, both from America and the rest of the world, decide to embark upon a dangerous journey to begin a new life in this foreboding land? Source 2 lists many of the factors that encouraged people to reject the idea of the Great American Desert and venture into this land. Use these examples to explore the different motives of the people who transformed the area out of all recognition.

SOURCE 3

Within a few exciting years the entire West had been settled, and all of the Great American Desert had been organised into territories and states.

W. E. Hollon, The Great American Desert, 1966.

Had this now become the Great American Garden?

SOURCE 2

	Reason	Example
1	Fertile land	'We came to a meadow so wide that its western rim touched the sky...The plain was covered with grass tall as ripe wheat.' *H. Garland, A Son of the Middle Border.*
2	Cheap land	'The deciding motive . . . was the lure of land that could be had practically without money.' *N. H. Letts and T. Allen, Narratives, 1823–63.*
3	Better life	Source 4 shows a painting by Mort Kunstler called 'Movement West'.
4	Government encouragement	'The United States government encouraged settlers to move West, for the more Americans living in an area, the better the government's opportunity for taking over it.' *Virginia Hopkins, Pioneers of the Old West, 1988.*
5	Inspired by the trailblazers	'They firmly believed that they could not fail in their endeavours; and they combined optimism and enthusiasm.' *Gerald Kreyche, Visions of the American West, 1989.*
6	Lure of gold and silver	'THE GOLD REGION IN CALIFORNIA! STARTLING DISCOVERIES!... We now have the highest official authority for believing in the discovery of vast gold mines in California.' **New York Herald, December 1848**
7	Employment	'I had always wanted to be a real cowboy.' *Jim Herron, 1880.*

8	Escape poverty and persecution	'Are you glad to be settled in the West?' 'Oh yes, very glad, a thousands times better here . . . Because here I am free.' *German emigrant, 1850s.*
9	Religion	Mormons went to escape persecution. 'Why did the Mormons arouse such hostility? . . . Most felt that its beliefs were superstitious, disgusting, repellent.' *L. Arrington and D. Bitton,* **The Mormon Experience***, 1979.*
10	Better transport	Several emigrant routes grew up. Later came the railroads. 'Emigrants would flock upon it as pigeons to their roosts . . . and spring into existence the long line of houses, of towns and villages . . . and all that civilisation offers.' *Congressman T. H. Benton.*
11	Newspaper reports	Newspapers made extravagant claims. 'Is it a good country for corn, you ask? Stranger, you'll never know what corn is until you go to Kansas.' *Newspaper article, 1886.*
12	Escape taxation	'You need to work as hard here as in any part of the world, but elsewhere it is to pay taxes, whereas, here it buys a farm.' *Emigrant from Wales, 1850s.*
13	Over-population in the East	'The area was getting so crowded that often one settler could see another neighbour's land.' *G. Kreyche,* **Visions of the American West***, 1989.*
14	Disease	'Epidemics of sickness also drove people West, where both legend and logic suggested the airs were purer.' *H. Horn,* **The Pioneers***, 1974.*
15	Start over again	'The frontier attracted a great many misfits . . . thieves, conmen, fugitives . . . and prostitutes. Perhaps these people saw the West as an opportunity to leave their past behind and start over . . . an opportunity to take advantage of a lawless wilderness.' *Virginia Hopkins,* **Pioneers of the Old West***, 1988.*

SOURCE 4

The 'Movement West' by Mort Kunstler.

1. What does 'The Great American Desert' mean?
2. Describe its features and climate.
3. What does Source 3 tell us about what happened?

4. a) Draw up the following table and put each of the reasons into the appropriate column. You can put some in more than one column if appropriate.

Factors for moving west

Push			Pull		
Political	Economic	Social	Political	Economic	Social

   b) What do your results show?
5. Explain, using examples, what were the main factors for people going West.

TO OREGON!

One of the most popular destinations for settlers moving west in the 1840s was Oregon, in the north-west. The trail there was tough (Source 1). Why did thousands of Americans risk their lives to go on this daunting 3,200km journey over the Rocky Mountains when 10% of them would die during it?

Oregon was a sensitive area: it was claimed by the USA, Great Britain, and even Spain until 1819. There was an urgency to get as many Americans in it as possible to strengthen the US claim, as there were only 150 of them by 1840. By 1843 the wagons were rolling, with over 10,000 having gone by 1846. By 1869 more than half a million people had made the journey: it was little wonder that this became known as 'Oregon Fever'.

The most popular place for departure was Independence in May. Emigrants risked their lives if they chose an early departure time as there was insufficient grass for animals. Early wagon trains included between 20 to 30 families, though this rose to 200 wagons. The departure could be chaotic with so many people, several of whom could not even control their animals! The account in Source 2 gives little idea of the forthcoming hardships.

SOURCE 1

Sections of the Oregon Trail had been used by the Native Americans and trappers. As early as 1742, part of the trail in Wyoming had been blazed by a Canadian explorer . . . The Lewis and Clark expedition, between 1804 and 1806, made more of it known . . . Later, mountain men . . . contributed their knowledge of the trail and often acted as guides.

Encarta, Microsoft CD-Rom, 1998.

SOURCE 2

Shops had sprung up to furnish emigrants with necessaries for the journey. The streets were thronged with men, horses and mules. There was an incessant hammering and banging from a dozen blacksmiths' sheds, where the heavy wagons were being repaired, and the horses and oxen shod . . . A train of emigrant wagons from Illinois passed through – a multitude of healthy children's faces were peeking out from under the covers of the wagons.

Francis Parkman, The Oregon Trail, 1847.

SOURCE 3

ON THE OREGON TRAIL

Transport

Speed
About 3 km an hour on flat ground
Travelled about 16 - 32 km a day.

Wagons
Small with rounded bottom to stop goods falling out. Cotton cover treated with linseed oil
Carried 450 - 675 kg.

Animals
Oxen - best, slow but sure, with stamina
Mules - faster but less stamina, bad-tempered
Horses - could not live on Prairie grass

Routine

Morning
Rose at 4am. Breakfast at 5am and set off
Scouts went ahead

Mid-day
Rested for lunch at 11am. Resumed at 2pm.

Night
Continued until nearly 10pm.
Most slept under their wagons

Hazards

Indian attacks
Not common until 1860s

River crossings
Many drowned

Sickness
Including cholera, dysentery and gunshot wounds (usually accidents)

Supplies

Food
Including: flour, bacon, dried fruit, sugar, coffee, milk (brought cows with them)

Medicines
Included laudanum made from opium to make sufferers feel better

Equipment
Including: tool box, buckets, water barrel, tar and grease

SOURCE 6

'On the Oregon Trail' by Albert Bierstadt, 1869.

The journey lasted between four and six months (Source 3). Most families packed their wagons so full that they had to walk: even so, many had to jettison some of their goods. Rules were drawn up with a captain in charge of a wagon train, and serious offences could be punished by expulsion which meant almost certain death. The dangers and misery people faced is summed up in these horrific examples (Source 4).

SOURCE 4

'We camped at a place where a woman had been buried and the wolves dug her up. Her hair was there with a comb still in it. She had been buried too shallow. It seems a dreadful fate, but what is the difference.'

Agnes Stewart.

'We had to kill Cash the dog and eat him. We ate his entrails and feet and hide and everything about him . . . 10 starved to death . . . 3 died and the rest ate them . . . I have not told you half of the trouble we had but I have written enough to let you know that you don't know what trouble is.'

Elizabeth Read.

Emigrants could pick up supplies at places such as Fort Laramie and Fort Bridger, though prices were high. Eventually a decision had to be made: continue to Oregon over peaks of 4,250m; or turn south and go to California. Most chose to continue to Oregon. A major consequence of this was to make the British hand over the territory to the US. In 1852 the territory was split into Oregon and Washington: Oregon was admitted to the Union in 1859, Washington in 1889.

The Trail's importance declined after 1869 with the first transcontinental railroad. However, its importance in history is reflected in Source 5.

SOURCE 5

The Oregon Trail was . . . the only practical corridor to the entire western United States. The places we now know as Washington, Oregon, California, Nevada, Idaho and Utah would probably not be a part of the United States today were it not for the Oregon Trail. That's because the Trail was the only feasible way for settlers to get across the mountains. Without the Trail, most of the American West would likely be a part of Canada or Mexico today.

The Oregon Trail Internet Site, 1997.

1. Describe the early exploration of the Trail according to Source 1.
2. a) Why did the US Government want people to go to Oregon?

   b) How successful was this?
3. What effect did the Trail have on the ownership of Oregon territory?
4. Explain what life was like on the Trail.

5. Use Sources 3 to 6 and the text to explain what discomforts and problems emigrants faced on their journey.
6. Why did thousands of Americans risk their lives to go on this journey?

GOLD!

Group 1 : The mining

In January 1848 James Marshall was working at his employer's new mill near Sutter's Fort, California. He noticed sparkles in the mud: the sparkle of gold! He told his employer, John Sutter, who tried to keep this discovery a secret. He failed: within two years 40,000 people had descended on Central California hoping to make themselves rich. They became known as the 'Forty Niners'. This unit invites you to judge this so-called 'gold rush'. Was the gold rush a success?

In the early days gold was easy to find by panning with a sieve in a river to sort out the gold from sand and water. Gold is 19 times heavier than water and four times heavier than sand, so stayed at the bottom of the pan. Regulations were set out to make claims: anyone not working his claim for a period of time would lose it. Often, however, in absence of anybody to enforce the law, men took things into their own hands, with occasional lynchings. Early miners got up to $20 a day, but as more people arrived, so the pickings dwindled until panning was not worth the trouble. New machines were introduced, with blasting and drilling now necessary, and individuals found themselves having to work for large companies to survive in conditions that could be grim. In the mines temperatures often exceeded 55°C.

Even so, more and more people flocked to the area both to mine and to work in the service industries: in San Francisco 25,000 Chinese had arrived by 1852 making up 10% of the state's population. Other cities such as Virginia City and Sacramento grew rapidly. If a gold strike lasted more than three months a settlement soon followed, making large sums of money for a few as miners found themselves paying huge sums of money for many items and services.

This led to unimaginable wealth for some. Between 1851 and 1855 the USA produced nearly 45% of the world's gold. It produced $81 million worth in 1852 alone! This later fell as supplies decreased. So the miners went elsewhere, making substantial claims during the rest of the century including:

- 1860s   Montana and Wyoming
- 1870s   Black Hills, Dakota
- 1880s   Idaho
- 1890s   Yukon.

Now study these sources and judge for yourself the success of the California gold rush.

SOURCE 1

24 - James Marshall finds gold at Sutter's Mill
28 - Marshall tells John Sutter about find

15 - newspaper *The Californian* publishes article about the find

14 - newspaper *The Star* stops publication as so many left for the gold rush
25 - proclamation against large number of army deserters gone to the gold rush

12 - gold found at new site beyond Sutter's Mill
20 - *The Californian* stops publication as readership crashed as so many went to the mines

19 - *New York Herald* announces news to the world

5 - President Polk makes reference to the gold rush in his address to Congress

Jan Feb Mar Ap May Jun Jul Aug Sep Oct Nov Dec

1848 Gold Rush

SOURCE 2

Now I will tell you what we have done since we got here: we have worked eight hour days and have made $16,000 . . . Board is worth $10 a day, and rough at that. There are a great many in the gold diggings at work, some are making fortunes and some are spending fortunes. A man who will half work can make great fortune in three years . . . My advice to you is to come and make your fortune while it is plenty, but leave your family.

Letter from two Missourians, 1849.

SOURCE 3

Madness and anticipation filled the air everywhere. It affected all classes, well-born and workers alike . . . Miners and prospectors were the same no matter what their country of origin . . . No one caught the new yellow fever like Americans, however, for gambling was as American as apple pie.

Gerald F. Kreyche, Visions of the American West, *1989.*

SOURCE 4

The time of miracles is past. The sweetest illusions are lost. . . . The awakening is all the more terrible as the dreams had been so glittering. From a distance California appears all golden. From closer at hand, the gold disappears . . . Homesickness grips these poor people. They . . . detest the gold, the mines, and their own destiny. Half of the miners are at that point today.

Etienne Derbec, French correspondent, 1850.

SOURCE 5

The most likely calculation is that about $1 million remained in California, most of it in the possession of Sam Brannan and other merchants. Nearly half of the gold was shipped to Chile and Peru in exchange for goods, another $400,000 went to the East Coast, and $300,000 to the British. The remainder floated through the Golden Gate to such outposts of trade as Honolulu, Panama, and Mexico. The bulk of California's first gold harvest now rested in the vaults of foreign businessmen.

Donald Dale Jackson, Gold Dust, *1980.*

SOURCE 7

Painting of hydraulic mining by Mrs J. Brown, Idaho State. The blasting effect of the water led to extensive environmental damage, such as huge amounts of top soil getting into rivers.

Group 2 : Social and economic effects

SOURCE 8

Many men came in, Sunday after Sunday, and gambled off all the gold they had dug during the week, having to get credit at a store for their next week's provisions, and returning to their diggings to work for six days in getting more gold, which would all be transferred the next Sunday to the gamblers, in the vain hope of recovering what had already been lost.

There were many drunken men, and consequently frequent rows and quarrels. Almost every man wore a pistol or knife – many wore both – but they were rarely used. The liberal and prompt administration of lynch law had done a great deal towards checking the wanton and indiscriminate use of these weapons on any slight occasion.

J. D. Borthwick, Three Years in California, *1857.*

SOURCE 6

Painting of gold panning, California, 1869.

SOURCE 9

San Francisco was beginning to resemble a battlefield hospital. By mid-October (1848) the pale and weakened victims of various fevers were coming into the city by the launch-load . . . The few available doctors charged an ounce or more for a visit.

Donald Dale Jackson, Gold Dust, *1980.*

SOURCE 10

A stroll through the village revealed the extent to which ordinary comforts of life were achievable. The gambling-houses, of which there were three or four, were of course the largest buildings; their mirrors, chandeliers, and other decorations, suggesting a style of life at odds with everything around them.

J. D. Borthwick, Three Years in California, *1857.*

SOURCE 14

Photograph of a mining town: Central City, Deadwood Gulch, Dakota, 1876. There are few trees in the background because of environmental damage caused by mining.

SOURCE 11

Then the people commenced rushing up from San Francisco and other parts of California, in May 1848: in the former village only five men were left to take care of the women and children. The single men locked their doors and left . . .

What a great misfortune was this sudden gold discovery for me! . . . From my mill buildings I reaped no benefit whatever, the mill stones even have been stolen and sold. My tannery, which was then in a flourishing condition, and was carried on very profitably, was deserted . . . Even the Indians . . . commenced to have some gold to buy all kinds of articles at enormous prices in the stores. When my Indians saw this, they wished very much to go to the mountains and dig gold.

John A. Sutter, 1857. Despite his involvement in the first discovery, Sutter's businesses lost a fortune. He failed in his bid to get compensation from the Government.

SOURCE 12

Prices . . . remained high. John Banks rented a saw and an axe for $2 a day apiece. A pair of socks set him back $1.50. Cheese and raisins were £1.50 a pound (500g), potatoes and dried apples $1 . . . Hotel keeping was lucrative. Even with expenses of more than $2,000 a month, the manager of the largest hotel in Marysville calculated that he could clear from $15,000 to $20,000 in six months.

Donald Dale Jackson, Gold Dust, *1980.*

SOURCE 13

The social effects of gold rushes spread widely. Storekeepers had to be supplied with goods, of course. Urban centres, freighting, shipbuilding, and the merchant marine felt the boom . . . In California fortunes were made by men who could corner markets in crucial items.

Robert V. Hine, The American West, *1984.*

SOURCE 15

Picture of San Francisco. Its population rose from 14,000 in 1848 to 380,000 by 1860.

1. Use Source 1 to write an account of what happened in 1848.

2. a) What was gold panning?

   b) Explain how this changed as gold supplies dwindled in the rivers.

3. What effect had the gold rush on the development of settlements?

4. Explain how 'this led to unimaginable wealth for some'.

5. What other places experienced major gold discoveries?

Stage 1. Copy out and fill in this table.

Source	Evidence supporting its success	Source	Evidence against its success

Stage 2. a) Write up the argument supporting the success of the gold rush. Refer to the sources to supply evidence.

b) Repeat for the argument against.

Stage 3. Your judgement: Was the gold rush a success?

HOMESTEADERS ON THE GREAT PLAINS

Even if you did travel West, how could ordinary Americans get a slice of the millions of acres of land on which to start their new life? The answer lay with the US Government which owned most of the land and which was happy to sell off this land for only $1.25 an acre. In 1841 the government had passed the Pre-emption Act to protect the land from being bought by greedy speculators. However, this was poorly enforced. Also, many poorer people could not afford this cheap land.

The solution was the 1862 Homestead Act, approved by President Lincoln and passed by Congress after a lot of argument (Source 1). Anyone could claim 160 acres of land: this land was free – the only costs were administration ones of around $10. Conditions were laid down to ensure people used the land for themselves before they could own it (Source 2).

SOURCE 2

We took out homesteads directly . . . As it is, we must live on it for five years. The first two years we live 'off and on' – that is, we must sleep on it once in a while and make some improvements on it within six months, or it will be forfeited. It is to be our home.

Howard Ruede, 1877.

However, the Homestead Act only applied to land that had been officially surveyed – large areas had not. Much was still sold rather than given free – three to four times the amount. Another restriction was that land taken from the Indians was not available under the Act. All of this allowed a lot of unscrupulous activities. Source 3 shows one way round the regulation that a house must be at least '12 by 14'! Speculators managed to buy up extensive areas as enforcement remained weak. Also, as the good land was already settled, many were forced to accept very poor land that required a huge amount of it to make a living. Twentieth-century historians have been generally positive about the Homestead Act (Source 4).

SOURCE 4

A) With all its shortcomings the Homestead Act clearly has more to its credit than any other one land act passed by the federal government . . . It was a means of peopling the wilderness.

Benjamin H. Hibbard, A History of the Public Land Policies, 1939.

B) The dream had become law, and for a hundred years Americans would believe that if things went bad, they could move west and take up a free homestead.

Robert V. Hine, The American West, 1984.

SOURCE 1

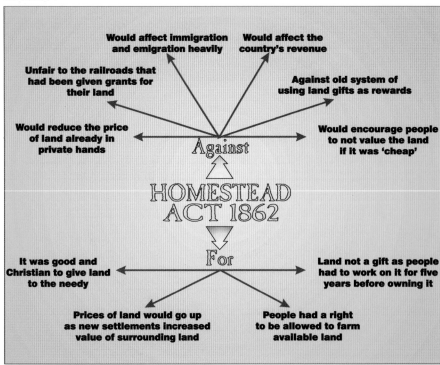

22

SOURCE 3

Cartoon about a house '12 by 14'.

The Homestead Act was followed up by several others.

- **1873 – Timber and Culture Act.** Homesteaders could have an additional 160 acres provided 40 acres were planted with trees.

- **1877 – Desert Land Act.** This offered another 640 acres at $1.25 an acre provided some of it was irrigated.

- **1878 – Timber and Stone Act.** Homesteaders could buy 160 acres of land that was unfit for cultivation, but valuable for stone and timber, for $2.50 an acre.

Some people found these extra opportunities difficult to put into practice (Source 5).

SOURCE 5

The timber filing requires a man to break 10 acres the first year, which he must plant with trees 12 feet (3.6m) apart the second year, besides breaking an additional 10 acres. The third year he must plant these 10, and break 20, which must be planted the fourth year. Then he is entitled to an additional 160 acres. It is a hard thing to live up to the law on a timber filing because young trees are hard to get, and when you have them, the question is whether they will grow.

Howard Ruede, 1877.

Despite problems these Acts were successful and people flocked to the West (Source 6). This led to the development of 'Bonanza' farms. By 1880 there were nearly 3,000 of these large farms of more than 1,000 acres each in the nine north-central states and territories, using the latest technology (see pages 42–43).

SOURCE 6

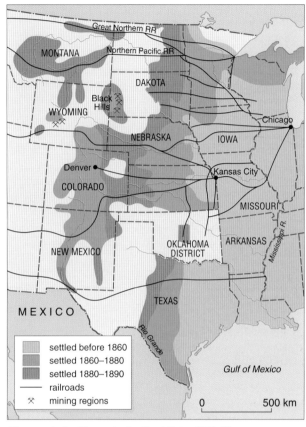

	settled before 1860
	settled 1860–1880
	settled 1880–1890
—	railroads
⚒	mining regions

0   500 km

Movement of settlers onto the Great Plains, 1860–90.

1. Explain the importance of these dates: 1841; 1862; 1873; 1877; 1878.

2. a) What regulations were included to ensure land went to deserving people?

   b) Were these successful?

3. Study Source 6. Describe what this shows about the spread of homesteaders.

4. Which set of arguments in Source 1 is most convincing? Explain your choice.

5. How far do Sources 3 and 5 prove that Government land policy was unsuccessful?

6. 'The Homestead Act was one of the most important reasons for the development of the West.' Do you agree? Give examples to support your argument.

COMMUNICATIONS

Horse power

Efficient transport is something we take for granted. Without it we could not enjoy our modern lifestyles: from holidays abroad, to exotic fruit in supermarkets. Without efficient transport the colonisation of the American West could not have happened. The West's success depended upon getting people, goods and information to and from it as quickly as possible. The conquest of distance was one of the greatest achievements of the period.

There were many early attempts to organise the transport of goods and people, especially after the discovery of gold in California in 1848. This ranged from a post office service between prospectors and their families at 5 cents for distances under 480km, to long distance land routes linking the East and West. This was especially needed as freight and mail bound for California went by sea: if this were via South America the journey would take six months! Several routes were developed, the main ones being:

- 3,200km Oregon Trail in the North (Source 1);
- 1,300km Santa Fe Trail in the South (see Source 1 and pages 14–15).

SOURCE 1

Pony Express overland route and various trails.

SOURCE 2

Pony Express: first rider leaving St Joseph, Missouri, 1860.

The Pony Express

The most exciting part of this development was the Pony Express between Missouri and California (Source 2). It only lasted for a mere 18 months from 1860, yet captured the imagination of Americans. Riders, usually aged between 18 and 20, rode in relays over a distance of just under 3,200km in ten days: a staggering achievement at this time. Well over 100 relay stations

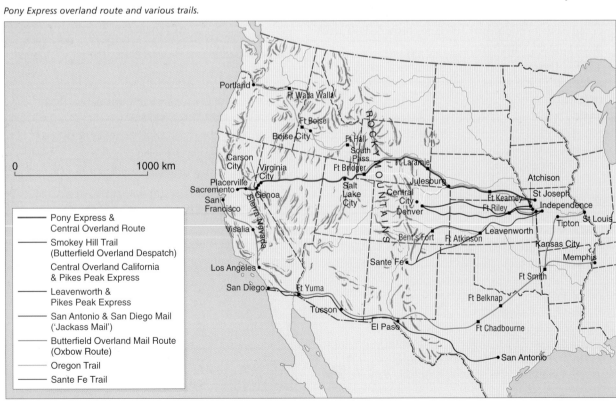

Pony Express & Central Overland Route
Smokey Hill Trail (Butterfield Overland Despatch)
Central Overland California & Pikes Peak Express
Leavenworth & Pikes Peak Express
San Antonio & San Diego Mail ('Jackass Mail')
Butterfield Overland Mail Route (Oxbow Route)
Oregon Trail
Sante Fe Trail

were set up, and around 120 young riders were employed to ride the relays of between 55 and 120 km. The journey took them through dangerous territory, made more dangerous as they were not allowed to carry a gun because of its weight. We are lucky to have an account written by the writer Mark Twain who gives us an indication of the operation (Source 3).

The mail they carried consisted of items such as letters, newspapers and telegrams written and printed on wafer-thin paper. However, it proved too costly: the service made losses of between $300,000 and $500,000 during its 18 months, and it had to be abandoned despite the widespread admiration it received.

SOURCE 3

The pony-rider was usually a little bit of a man, brimful of spirit and endurance. No matter what time of the day or night his watch came on, and no matter whether it was winter or summer, raining, snowing, hailing, or sleeting, or whether his 'beat' was a level straight road or a crazy trail over mountain crags and precipices, or whether it led through peaceful regions or regions that swarmed with hostile Indians, he must be always ready to leap into the saddle and be off like the wind!

Mark Twain.

SOURCE 4

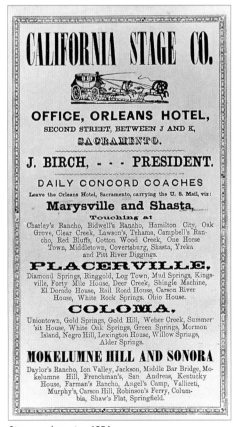

Stagecoach poster, 1854.

Stagecoaches

The age of the stagecoach arrived with companies competing for trade just like modern bus companies (Source 4). Just like today, this could be cutthroat. One small operator charging $6 for a 48km journey was put out of business by a giant company who charged $4. As soon as this company had a monopoly it put the price up to $12, doubled the journey times, and used poorer quality stagecoaches!

Stagecoaches could also carry valuable cargoes: one receipt that has been preserved is for $87,000 in notes and gold dust, with a fee of $930 for carrying it. Of all of the companies, the most famous was Wells Fargo which began in 1852, and got rid of all of its opposition within 15 years. By 1866 it had 196 offices and was famous throughout the West: the opening of a Wells Fargo office was a sign that a town was properly established. Another major player was the Butterfield Overland Mail that was named after John Butterfield who proved to be very enthusiastic but ran up huge debts despite a federal subsidy.

Travelling in stagecoaches was horrid. There were three rows of passengers: those in the middle row had nothing for support apart from leather straps suspended from the ceiling to protect them from the unending bumps. All had to sleep sitting upright. Clouds of dust got into the carriage and made conditions awful. Those in stagecoaches that climbed the Rockies found themselves on narrow paths with sheer drops down the mountainside. They arrived at their destinations totally exhausted: one passenger described it as the hardest two weeks of his life, and spent 20 hours in bed recovering!

1. Why were efficient communications so important in the development of the American West?

2. What were the two main land routes?

3. Explain the importance of:
   a) the Pony Express;
   b) stagecoaches.

4. i) What impression is the artist of Source 2 trying to make?
   ii) How does this compare with the impression in Source 3?

5. Study Source 4. How useful is this to historians finding out about travel in the American West?

Technology and the iron horse

One reason for the failure of the Pony Express was new technology. The British and Americans each pioneered the telegraph in 1837. The original system only allowed electrical signals to be carried about 30km; however, later improvements changed this and signals could be carried great distances far more quickly than the Pony Express. At the same time newspapers, such as William Randolph Hearst's *San Francisco Examiner*, were increasing in popularity, carrying everything from news to scandals. Improvements in printing in the 1880s, with quicker typesetting, expanded the industry further, bringing regional, national and international news to the settlers of the West.

However, it was another technological invention that allowed the settlement of the West: the railroad. Americans took up the work of British pioneers George and Robert Stephenson to master the huge distances they had to travel, to create a network of thousands of kilometres of track across the continent, through gorges and over mountain ranges (Source 6).

SOURCE 6

This is the story of the first transcontinental railroad – the greatest, most daring engineering effort the country had yet seen . . . Imagine the task . . . to build a railroad across two-thirds of the continent and some of the most difficult terrain on earth . . . Not in all that distance, not in 1,700 miles [2,700 km] was there a single settlement of any appreciable size except at Salt Lake. The railroad would join what essentially were two different countries: California and back East. Construction crews would cross hundreds of miles of desert, push into the mountains at elevations as high as 8,000 feet [2,400m]. It's hard to believe that one river alone, the Weber, would have to be crossed 31 times. And all this without benefit of bulldozers, or rock drills, or modern explosives, or modern medical facilities.

Union Pacific Internet Site, 1997.

Planning the railroad

President Lincoln signed the Pacific Railroad Act in 1862 authorising two companies to build a transcontinental railway. People in the North wanted it built there, whilst Southerners wanted it near them. In the end the Civil War in the South meant it had to be built further north. Significantly, the Indians were not consulted even though the railroad would run through their lands. The Central Pacific was to build eastwards from Sacramento, California, whilst the Union Pacific was to build westwards from Omaha, Nebraska. They were to meet somewhere in the middle still to be arranged! Each company was given free land on 16km either side of the railroad line: in 1864 this was doubled. They were also paid for each mile of track they laid:

- $16,000 on flatland;
- $32,000 on intermediate plateaux;
- $48,000 in mountains.

Even with these grants, getting money was always a problem. Some saw the future benefits of the railroad, such as the Ames brothers from Boston who invested over $1 million in the project although they nearly went bankrupt. On one occasion President Lincoln was persuaded to agree that the Sierra Nevada Mountains began 40km before they did to allow the company more dollars per mile! Finally, just before the official 1869 opening, Thomas Durant, Vice-President of the Union Pacific, was kidnapped by unpaid workers who refused to release him until they were paid.

Building the line

Both companies had problems recruiting men. The Union Pacific hired thousands of Europeans, especially Irish, plus veterans of the Civil War – often blacks – at a rate of about $1 a day. The Central Pacific had particular problems as thousands were flocking to the gold mines rather than the railroad lines. This problem was solved by hiring many Chinese (Source 7).

SOURCE 7

Unlike the volatile Irish, the Chinese were not inclined to strike, did not get drunk on pay-day, did not frequent whorehouses in the mining towns along the C.P. [Central Pacific] right of way and did not lean on the pick handle when the boss was not looking. They did have the outrageous habit of bathing every day and they did drink enormous quantities of boiled tea – which did not make them sick the way carelessly quaffed ditchwater frequently afflicted white labourers.

K. Wheeler, The Railroaders, 1973.

Working conditions were often extreme: from baking deserts to the frozen winter Rocky Mountains. Even getting wood for track sleepers on the Great Plains was a feat in itself. Building was hampered by Indian attacks that only hastened the destruction of the Indians as more and more effort was put into destroying them (Source 8).

SOURCE 8

Every mile had to be run within range of the musket, as there was not a moment's security. In making the surveys numbers of our men, some of them the ablest and most promising, were killed . . . We've got to clean the Indian out, or give up.

Grenvelle Dodge, the Union Pacific's chief engineer.

Testing a span at Weber Canyon, 1869.

Tunnels were cut through solid rock in the mountains. One tunnel in the Sierra Nevada Mountains was cut through 500m of granite, 2,110m above sea level. Using blasting powder, work progressed at 20cm a day.

In the winter of 1866–67 workers had to contend with 44 blizzards, one lasting 13 days. Source 9 shows an incredible achievement: the testing of a span at Weber Canyon, Utah in 1869. This was particularly important as an earlier one had been swept away by floods.

SOURCE 10

The meeting of the two lines at Promontory, Utah. 'Driving the Golden Spike' by H. Charles McBarron, 1869.

Eventually the two lines met at the newly arranged site of Promontory, Utah, in May 1869. The last spike to be hammered home was made of gold, but the Central Pacific dignitary hitting it home managed to miss it with his blow (Source 10)! It was now possible to leave New York and be in San Francisco in 10 days.

Travelling on the railroad

In its first full year in 1870 15,000 passengers travelled on the railroad: this was a tiny number compared to the million who travelled in 1882. Those who could afford it travelled first class with all the luxuries possible over four days. At the other end, it was mainly

SOURCE 11

Conditions on a train in the 1870s.

emigrants who paid out $40 to travel third class on narrow wooden benches, and on much slower trains taking at least ten days. Source 11 shows the misery of travelling at night for most travellers. The writer Robert Louis Stephenson recorded his memories of travelling by train (Source 12).

SOURCE 12

I suppose the reader has some notion of an American railroad-car, that long, narrow wooden box, like a flat-roofed Noah's ark, with a stove and a convenience, one at either end, a passage down the middle, and transverse benches upon either hand. Those destined for emigrants on the Union Pacific are only remarkable for their extreme plainness . . . The benches are too short for anything but a young child . . . There were meals to be had by the wayside . . . Many conductors will hold no communication with an emigrant . . .

We were at sea on the plains of Nebraska . . . It was a world almost without a feature; an empty sky, an empty earth; front and back, the line of railway stretched from horizon to horizon, like a cue across a billiard-board.

Robert Louis Stephenson.

SOURCE 13

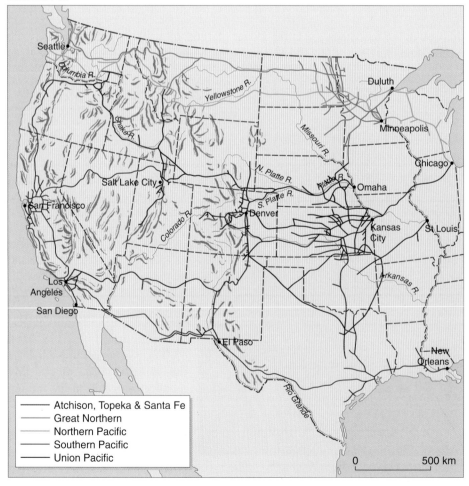

Seattle
Columbia R.
Yellowstone R.
Duluth
Snake R.
Minneapolis
Salt Lake City
N. Platte R.
Chicago
San Francisco
S. Platte R.
Platte R.
Omaha
Colorado R.
Denver
Kansas City
St Louis
Los Angeles
Arkansas R.
San Diego
El Paso
New Orleans
Rio Grande

—— Atchison, Topeka & Santa Fe
—— Great Northern
—— Northern Pacific
—— Southern Pacific
—— Union Pacific

0   500 km

Main railroad lines in the West.

Growth of the railroads

Over the next few decades the American West became criss-crossed with railroads (Sources 13 and 14). By the end of the century there were five main lines. Companies spent huge sums attracting the public not simply to travel on their routes, but to move out West. The Union Pacific spent $800,000 on advertising alone in 1874: Source 15 shows an early advert. By 1880 93,000 miles of lines had been constructed, soaring to 164,000 in the 1890s. Industries spread to the West with coal, iron and steel carried by the railroads along with foodstuffs and manufact-ured goods. What were luxuries now became necessities for some households. All along the railroad lines towns sprung up at about 100km intervals, whilst towns not on railroad lines often became deserted. John Quincy Adams of the Union Pacific summed it up: 'The simple truth was that through its energetic railroad development, the country was producing real wealth as no country ever produced before.'

SOURCE 14

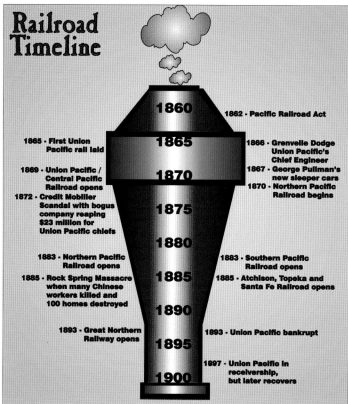

Railroad Timeline

- 1860
- 1862 · Pacific Railroad Act
- 1865 · First Union Pacific rail laid
- 1865
- 1866 · Grenville Dodge Union Pacific's Chief Engineer
- 1869 · Union Pacific / Central Pacific Railroad opens
- 1867 · George Pullman's new sleeper cars
- 1870
- 1870 · Northern Pacific Railroad begins
- 1872 · Credit Mobilier Scandal with bogus company reaping $23 million for Union Pacific chiefs
- 1875
- 1880
- 1883 · Northern Pacific Railroad opens
- 1883 · Southern Pacific Railroad opens
- 1885 · Rock Spring Massacre when many Chinese workers killed and 100 homes destroyed
- 1885
- 1885 · Atchison, Topeka and Santa Fe Railroad opens
- 1890
- 1893 · Great Northern Railway opens
- 1893 · Union Pacific bankrupt
- 1895
- 1897 · Union Pacific in receivership, but later recovers
- 1900

SOURCE 15

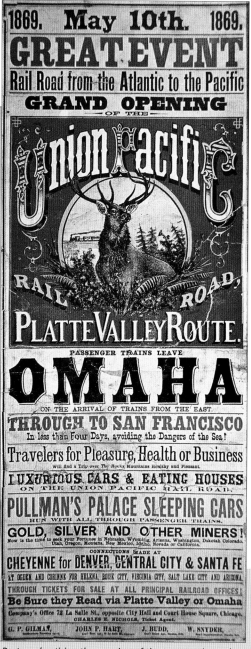

Poster advertising the opening of the transcontinental railroad, 10 May 1869.

1. How would the telegraph and newspapers improve communications in the West?

2. What were the main points of the 1862 Pacific Railroad Act?

3. Copy out and fill in:

Building the railroads

Type of problem	Example

4. What happened in May 1869?

5. What were conditions for passengers like in these early trains?

6. a) Using Source 14, make a list of the five major railroads and their completion dates?

   b) What information is there in Sources 13 and 14 to show that building the railroads was difficult?

7. Why were photographs 9 and 10 taken?

8. Study Sources 11 and 12.

   a) Why do you think conditions were so poor for all but first-class travellers?

   b) Why did people put up with these conditions?

9. Study Source 15. What did the Union Pacific hope to achieve by this poster campaign?

10. 'The railroad was the key to the development of the American West.' Do you agree?

AGE OF THE COWBOY: THE CATTLE BUSINESS

Why did the rearing of cattle turn into a big business during the second half of the 19th century? It not only brought incredible wealth to some, but created a collection of stories and legends still firing people's imaginations today. This unit explores the causes and consequences of the cattle business.

Beginnings

Cattle rearing originated in Mexico with the 'vacqueros'. They were the predecessors of the cowboys: indeed their name comes from the Spanish for cow. These men acquired remarkable skills. Source 1 shows vacqueros herding the cattle that were to play a crucial role in the trade of the American West: the famous longhorns. With horns up to 2.1m long, and a mean nature, these cattle needed highly skilled men to handle them. A modern cowboy writes about them in Source 2.

SOURCE 2

From the original Spanish stock emerged a hardy, rugged animal possessed of great stamina, an ability to survive with little water and sometimes on meagre feed. Surprisingly, these animals acquired two unique features – great size and tremendous horns . . . There has been no beast quite like it before or since.

Royal B. Hassrick, Cowboys, 1974.

The situation changed dramatically in 1845 when Texas became part of the Union and many Mexicans were hounded out. More Americans came to the area to work in the cattle trade. In 1848 there were 350,000 cattle in Texas: by 1855 that figure was over a million.

The second factor that boosted the cattle industry was the Civil War. By its end in 1865 the South was in

SOURCE 1

'Cattle Drive', a painting by James Walker, 1877.

ruins. Men returning to their lands discovered that their cattle had bred beyond belief: about 6 million longhorns were roaming free. Cattlemen could only get about $3–$4 a head at home, but in the North animals could fetch $30–$40 each. Huge profits could be made if cattle could be moved to the northern markets where the population was growing rapidly. So the long drive was born.

SOURCE 3

Suddenly, the right conditions fell into place like the tumblers in a combination lock: the Civil War brought an increased demand for beef; a humid cycle brought increased rainfall to the Great Plains; settlers learned that cattle could thrive on the native grass and survive the drastic changes in climate; the transcontinental railroads pushed to the Pacific; and, finally, the great buffalo herds on which the Plains' Indians economy had depended were destroyed and the Indians were confined to specific reservations.

W. E. Hollon, The Great American Desert, *1966.*

Development

Source 4 shows the main cattle trails that developed. Most were connected to railroad lines. The drive required good organisation and appropriate equipment (Source 5).

SOURCE 5

A typical trail-driving outfit consisted of 2,000 to 3,000 long-horn steers, a trail boss, eight cowpunchers, a cook, horse wrangler, about 65 ponies, and a four-horse chuck wagon that carried bedrolls and provisions of corn meal, sorghum, molasses, beans, salt, sugar, and coffee.

W. E. Hollon, The Great American Desert, *1966.*

Three thousand longhorns would make a cost effective drive. They would be purchased at about $8 each and sold for $20. This would result in a profit of $30,000 after taking expenses into account. Source 6 shows the huge growth in the trade.

Another consequence of this was the development of cowtowns. In 1867 Joseph McCoy decided that there had to be a place where Southern cattlemen and Northern buyers could meet to trade safely. McCoy saw the benefits of the new railroads and chose an obscure place called Abilene on the Kansas Pacific Railroad (Source 7).

SOURCE 7

Abilene was selected because the country was entirely unsettled, well watered, had excellent grass, and nearly the entire area of country was adapted to holding cattle. It was the farthest point east at which a good depot for cattle business could have been made . . . In sixty days from 1 July a shipping yard that would accommodate 3,000 cattle . . . was completed, and a good three-storey hotel well on the way towards completion.

Joseph McCoy.

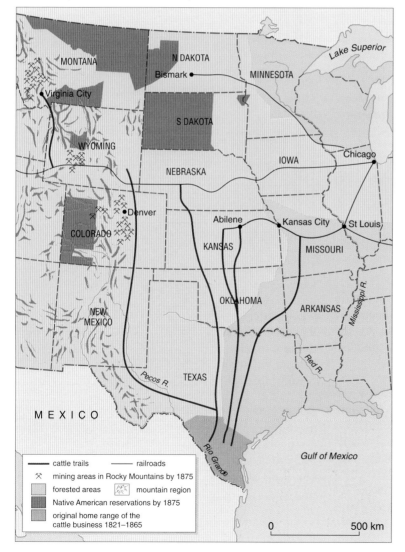

cattle trails — railroads
✕ mining areas in Rocky Mountains by 1875
forested areas — mountain region
Native American reservations by 1875
original home range of the cattle business 1821–1865
0   500 km

SOURCE 4

The main cattle trails.

SOURCE 6

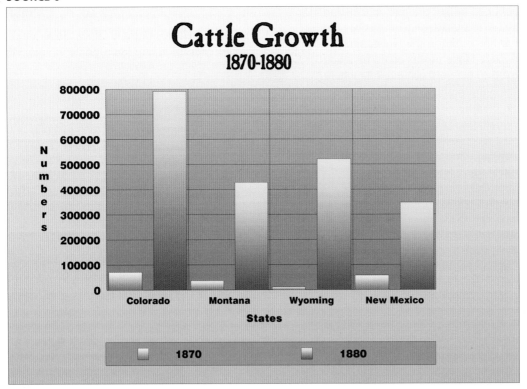

Cattle Growth
1870-1880

Abilene was 'the king of cowtowns' for five years: 35,000 cattle were brought there in 1867; by 1871 that figure had risen to 700,000. Eventually, many residents got sick of the riotous behaviour of some cowboys. They placed a notice in two newspapers:

SOURCE 8

We the undersigned . . . most respectfully request all who have contemplated driving Texas cattle to Abilene the coming season to seek some other point for shipment, as the inhabitants of Dickinson (County) will no longer accept the evils of the trade.

Remarkably this worked and the cattle trade moved to places such as Dodge City (see page 37). The economic consequences for Abilene were severe and by the spring of 1873 four-fifths of businesses were closed.

Cattle rearing was initially on open ranges: public domain land for all to use. Some people saw the benefits of buying some land near to rivers: by doing this they could control huge areas beyond, as land was worthless without water. This led to individuals capitalising on their land holdings and developing huge cattle ranches run by powerful cattle barons such as Charles Goodnight (see pages 74–75). Ranches of 1,000 square miles were not unusual, with cowboys

employed by the ranchers. Source 9 shows the centrepiece of one of these. Ranches tended to have vague borders agreed upon by neighbours. Along the boundaries there were occasional cabin stations, each with a couple of men to oversee the perimeter. To identify cattle each was branded. This was the 'cattle kingdom'.

Decline

This success was short-lived: its conclusion was to be the end of the open range. By the 1880s more breeders were experimenting with new breeds – especially English Herefords – to produce higher quality meat from the growing number of shorthorn cattle. This meat was in greater demand in the North where people were getting tired of tough longhorn meat. The new breeders objected to the open ranges that allowed diseased cattle to infect others. To regulate this, the Bureau of Animal Industry was created in 1884. Meanwhile the long drive was in decline (Source 10).

SOURCE 10

The business of driving Texas cattle northward is now confined to hardly more than a score of men, and these few men claim to make but a small margin of profit.

Western Kansas Cattle Growers' Association, 1884.

SOURCE 9

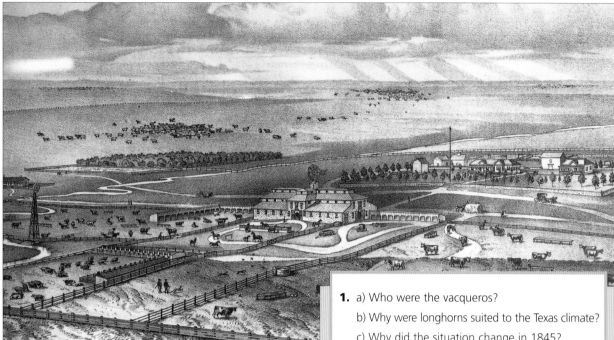

The ranch of J. P. Wiser & Son.

Another consequence of the development of the cattle industry was overproduction with too many cattle and no provision for any loss of feed. The appalling winter of 1886 showed the danger of this when ranchers lost 30% to 80% of their animals. From now on herds would have to be limited to make allowances for bad weather. In addition, resentment grew against large ranchers with a growth in cattle rustling. Many courts sympathised with the rustlers against the cattle barons and would not convict, even though rustling meant the death penalty if convicted. This was to lead to illegal violence and lynchings as we shall see later.

One major reason for change was technology. Railroads brought thousands of homesteaders who wanted to fence off their lands. Gilden's invention of barbed wire, and the new windpumps (see pages 42–43) helped destroy the long drives. Windpumps brought water to arid land and an influx of small farmers; whilst barbed wire was so plentiful that no matter how much was cut by cowboys, there was still more. In Source 11 a historian explains.

1. a) Who were the vacqueros?

    b) Why were longhorns suited to the Texas climate?

    c) Why did the situation change in 1845?

    d) How did the Civil War affect the cattle trade?

2. Study Source 4.

    a) What were the four main trails?

    b) Why do you think they all link up with railroads?

3. What does Source 5 tell us about their organisation and equipment?

4. a) Why was Abilene chosen as the first cattle town?

    b) How successful was it?

5. a) What were open ranges?

    b) What was a cattle baron?

    c) How large were ranches?

    d) How did neighbours keep their land and animals separated?

6. Explain how each of these led to the decline of open ranching:

    a) shorthorns; b) overproduction; c) resentment against ranchers; d) technology.

7. a) Under the title 'Causes' make a list of all the causes of the growth of the industry in your order of importance.

    b) Explain the reasons for your top choice.

8. Repeat question 7, this time under the title 'Consequences'.

9. 'A consequence of the development of the West was the deaths of the long drive and open ranch.' Do you agree?

SOURCE 11

The 'new' cattle kingdom was an empire of farmers possessing fenced, individually owned spreads equipped with sufficient shelter, feed, and water to resist a hostile climate. 'Scientific' beef producers replaced the cattlemen of old as cowboys became primarily posthole diggers and hay cutters. All would retain the wide-brimmed Stetson hat as a proud badge of their profession . . . but an era had come to an end.

Henry S. Commager (ed.), The American Destiny, *volume 9, 1976.*

Real cowboys

For many people, the cowboy is the most famous symbol of the American West. We have already seen how 20th-century myths have obscured the real cowboys. This unit develops this further and invites you to examine what cowboys really were like: were they the exciting heroes of Source 12, or the rather drab characters in Source 13? After you have studied the

SOURCE 13

Poor cowboys eat a meagre meal.

basic information in Source 14, you will study a range of written sources about them and their work.

SOURCE 12

'Cowboys roping a steer', a painting by Charles M. Russell, 1904.

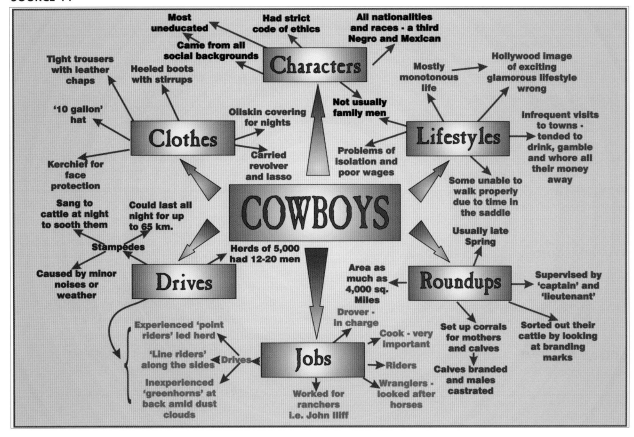

Secondary sources

These sources tell you what 20th-century historians believe cowboys were like, and how close this was to the myths that developed.

SOURCE 15

Even the first necessary of comfort was denied them. They were poorly dressed, and all armed to the last item . . . Yet . . . their simple and uncomplaining toughness and self-control, their dignity and their generous conduct to the younger members of the party left a lasting impression.

He rides day after day in rain or shine throughout the long season, collecting the cattle upon their wild pasture ground, and he is determined to meet all the hardships of one of the hardest jobs known to man. From May until November he may be in the saddle, each week growing gaunter and grimmer and more bronzed . . . If he be tired, none may know it; if he be sick, it shall not appear; if he be injured, it must not be confessed.

Emerson Hough, The Story of the Cowboy, *1954.*

SOURCE 16

The cowboy's life involved so much drudgery and loneliness and so little in the way of satisfaction that he drank to excess on his infrequent visits to the shoddy little cowtowns dotted over the West. A drifter whose work and economic status made it difficult for him to marry and rear a family, he sought female companionship among prostitutes. Most of his physical dangers scarcely bordered on the heroic . . . Rank and file cowboys were hired hands on horseback, and very unromantic ones at that.

Michael S. Kennedy (ed.), Cowboys and Cattlemen: A Roundup from Montana, *The Magazine of Western History, 1954.*

SOURCE 17

Walking was unnatural . . . The only sensible . . . form of locomotion was astride a horse. And while the bent-legged, hunchbacked cowboy could barely navigate on foot, on a horse he was transformed into a gallant, dashing hero.

Royal B. Hassrick, Cowboys, *1974.*

SOURCE 18

The cowboy's arduous way of life tended to develop rough-and-ready virtues, as well as extraordinary skills in horsemanship and marksmanship. These qualities have acquired an almost legendary character in numerous tales and songs, making the cowboy a traditional symbol of manliness.

Encarta, Microsoft CD-ROM, 1998.

SOURCE 19

He was made out of a mixture of men who were attracted to the frontier in search of adventure, and who came from nearly every type of family background, religion, and nationality.

Harold McCracken, The American Cowboy, *1973.*

SOURCE 20

On the great cattle drives, about one cowboy in six was black . . . But when the real Old West ended, the white mythmakers who were to carry its legend into the 20th century simply left the blacks out.

Paul O'Neil, The End and the Myth, *1979.*

Primary sources

These sources were either written or spoken by cowboys talking about their work, some decades later. How do these accounts compare with the impressions given by historians of what cowboys were like?

SOURCE 21

We had, during the night, four guards: first, second, third and fourth. These separate guards were on for two hours each. When the two hours were up one of the trio would go into camp and call the next guard. The last guards also called the cook, at the appointed hour which was very early, generally before daylight.

This 'standing guard', as night herding was called, was the hardest part of a cowboy's life . . . When the weather was bad, as in rain or sleet storm, a poor cowhand shivered all through his guard.

Bob Fudge, Recollections, *1932.*

SOURCE 22

There were about twenty of these Indians . . . Their chief did the talking to our Boss. He demanded one hundred of our best beef cattle, cut from the lead of the herd . . . The boss told him 'No'. He could have some from the drags . . . The Indians left at a gallop . . . The Boss had us corral the horses in our rope corral fastened to the wagon . . . We did not have to wait long for the Indians. . . When the Chief got within about one hundred yards of us he stopped his outfit and raised a white flag on a stick to show us he had accepted our terms . . . We all wondered why they had spared our lives.

Bob Fudge, Recollections, *1932. He discovered the next day that the Indians were on the run from the US army after killing some other Whites.*

SOURCE 23

I have seen day after day . . . an estimated 15,000 cattle on the roundup ground and where there were five wagons working together the roundup would be cut into five bunches. Each outfit would take a bunch and work and they would follow each other from one roundup to another until everybody was through. They would cut out the cow and calves first into a common bunch and a couple of cowboys would be sent to hold them on water until after supper at five o'clock. After supper, we branded, as we rarely got the roundup all thrown together until two o'clock and usually finished up working it around four or a little later.

J. K. Marsh, date unknown.

SOURCE 24

Running with them, you realise you are in front of the fear-crazed herd. Your life now depends on your horse. A fall in front of the rushing sea of cattle means death for both of you . . . You turn off at an angle to get to one side of the herd, then breathe a sigh of relief as you sense you are now running beside the herd instead of in its path.

You don't know where the other night herders are, but hope none of them have been mangled by the crazed cattle . . . After what seems eternity, you finally are riding in a circle around a bunch of milling cattle. They are exhausted. Soon they slow to a walk, then stop, sides heaving and tongues hanging out . . . So you continue to rise around tired cattle on a tired horse until the day begins to break.

Joe B. Franz, date unknown, on a stampede.

---

1. Use Source 14, plus any other information you have, to write up an account of cowboys under each of the six headings.

2. a) What advantages are there in using secondary sources to find out what real cowboys were like?

b) According to the secondary sources, what types of myths have grown up?

c) What problems can this cause?

3. a) In what ways are the primary sources better than secondary ones in finding out about real cowboys?

b) What problems can there be in using this type of primary evidence?

4. Were real cowboys like Source 12 or Source 13? Use this unit and any other knowledge you have to write a detailed answer.

Dodge City: Go to Hell!

Dodge City is still considered to be the best example of everything that was bad in the West, with its violence, alcohol, prostitutes and gambling. How far does Dodge City deserve this reputation?

SOURCE 25

A drunken cowboy got on the train . . . When the conductor asked his destination, the cowboy stated, 'I want to go to hell!' To this the conductor replied, 'All right; give me a dollar and get off at Dodge.'

Odie B. Faulk, Dodge City, 1977.

In 1872 a man put up a tent to sell whisky, and by that August the town of Dodge had begun, virtually in the middle of nowhere. Tent buildings became permanent and the town developed (Source 26). Initially, Dodge attracted buffalo hunters, but as buffalo numbers fell, cattlemen moved in from Abilene for their business and leisure. By 1877 there were 16 saloons selling 'whisky', which was little more than coloured raw alcohol with sometimes a rat or snake added for a fuller flavour! By 1879 there may have been 47 prostitutes: as men outnumbered women 6:1 they were always in demand. This was accompanied by disorder as there was no marshal until 1875: during its first year alone there were 15 killings.

However, many people in Dodge were decent and religious, and built the first church. A school was built in 1873. A literary society was formed, as were volunteer fire companies, and even a band. From the very beginning there were moves to end the bad behaviour in Dodge, and in the 1880s laws were passed to clean up Dodge and encourage more decent people to live there. This combined with a decline in ranching in the late 1880s (Source 27).

With this, Dodge passed from reality to myth, all within the space of a few years.

SOURCE 26

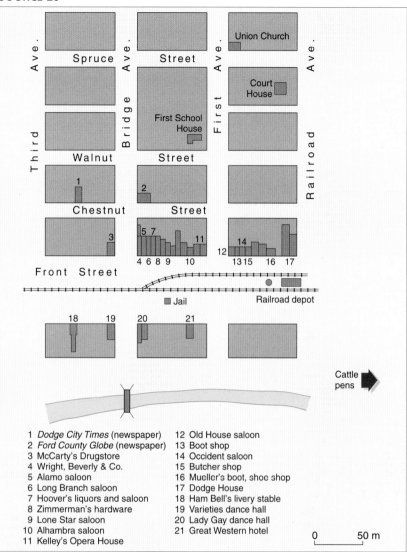

1 *Dodge City Times* (newspaper)
2 *Ford County Globe* (newspaper)
3 McCarty's Drugstore
4 Wright, Beverly & Co.
5 Alamo saloon
6 Long Branch saloon
7 Hoover's liquors and saloon
8 Zimmerman's hardware
9 Lone Star saloon
10 Alhambra saloon
11 Kelley's Opera House
12 Old House saloon
13 Boot shop
14 Occident saloon
15 Butcher shop
16 Mueller's boot, shoe shop
17 Dodge House
18 Ham Bell's livery stable
19 Varieties dance hall
20 Lady Gay dance hall
21 Great Western hotel

0   50 m

Street map of Dodge City.

SOURCE 27

The cowboy is already becoming conspicuous by his absence in Dodge . . . With the cowboy gone, the gamblers and prostitutes will find their occupations gone . . . The bulk of the saloons will then die out.

Judge Jeremiah, 1885.

1. What was the early town like?
2. Make a list of good and bad features of Dodge.

3. Does Source 27 suggest that Dodge was 'hell'?
4. The wild behaviour only lasted a few years. Why is this part of its history the best remembered?

THE PLIGHT OF THE INDIANS

This section has shown some of the vast changes that took place in the American West. In the middle of all this change were the Indians. We will now take a snapshot of the situation around 1850. Changes for white settlers had resulted in changes for the Indians that were to lead to the destruction of their civilisation. This process was helped by the belief among most white Americans that Indian culture was savage and should be destroyed. Source 1 shows Native American homelands in 1840 as the 'Frontier' edged West. The frontier was the line drawn by the US Government dividing US territory from the barren land thought fit only for Indians.

The effect of contact with whites was considerable, especially gaining the horse as we saw earlier. Now Indians received guns and the incentive to compete against each other for the lucrative business with white traders: this often led to violence and war. They were also given whisky, which was to help destroy their culture. Whites also passed on the scourge of diseases, especially smallpox, as Source 2 describes.

SOURCE 2

Four Bears never saw a White Man hungry . . . I was always ready to die for them . . . I have done everything that a Red Skin could do for them, and how they have repaid it! I do not fear Death my friends. You know it. But to die with my face rotten, that even the wolves will shrink with horror at seeing me . . . Rise all together and not leave one of them alive.

Four Bears, a Mandan chief.

SOURCE 1

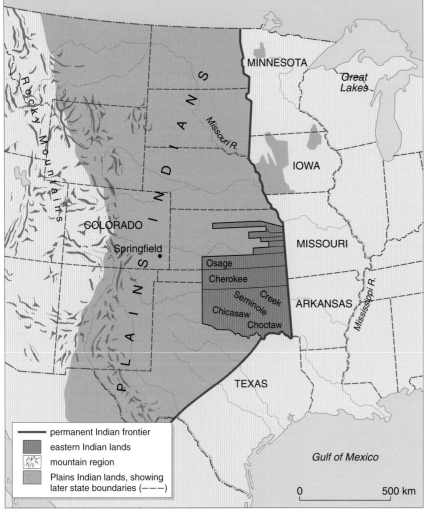

- permanent Indian frontier
- eastern Indian lands
- mountain region
- Plains Indian lands, showing later state boundaries (———)

0   500 km

The Frontier and Indian lands on the Great Plains in 1840.

The effect of disease on Indians was dreadful. Smallpox was at its worst at the end of the 18th century, especially as the Indians could do nothing to stop the spread of the disease. It returned in the 1830s with devastating effects: between 1837 and 1840 17,000 died. This was followed by cholera in 1849 that killed thousands more.

At the same time the numbers of white settlers moving west was on the increase as settlers ventured across the Great American Desert. The Oregon Trail worsened the situation.

SOURCE 4

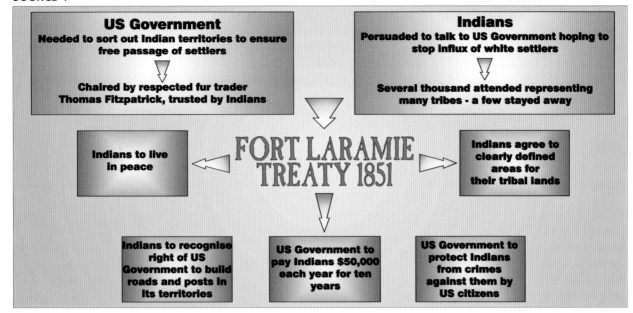

US Government
Needed to sort out Indian territories to ensure free passage of settlers
⇩
Chaired by respected fur trader Thomas Fitzpatrick, trusted by Indians

Indians
Persuaded to talk to US Government hoping to stop influx of white settlers
⇩
Several thousand attended representing many tribes - a few stayed away

FORT LARAMIE TREATY 1851

Indians to live in peace

Indians agree to clearly defined areas for their tribal lands

Indians to recognise right of US Government to build roads and posts in its territories

US Government to pay Indians $50,000 each year for ten years

US Government to protect Indians from crimes against them by US citizens

SOURCE 3

When the trail to Oregon was opened to wagon trains in the early 1840s, the resulting annual flow of travellers brought critical new problems to the Indian tribes . . . As the wagon trains increased in size and number each year, the friction between the travellers and the tribes along the trail soon built up to the danger point, and minor conflicts erupted all along the way. Most problems between red men and white resulted directly from the white man's firm belief that an Indian had no rights of any kind, even in his own land.

Francis Haines, The Plains Indians, 1976.

The situation deteriorated further when gold was discovered in California in 1848 (see pages 18–21) leading to a huge movement of white settlers across Indian land. These people helped to upset the buffalo herds that had grazed peacefully, but now fled as the settlers moved in. Attacks on settlers grew. One modern historian has said: 'It is a mystery why the Indians under such circumstances were so tolerant and why serious incidents were so few.' However, the white population demanded protection from the US Government. The 'Indian problem' was now placed in the hands of a government department: the Indian Bureau. This resulted in the Fort Laramie Treaty of 1851 (Source 4). For many people this was to be the solution to their problems (Source 5).

SOURCE 5

The happy results of this council are, no doubt, owing to the prudent measures of the commissioners of the Government . . . The council will doubtless produce the good effect they have the right to expect. It will be the commencement of a new era for the Indians – an era of peace. In future, peaceable citizens may cross the desert unmolested, and the Indian will have little to dread from the bad white man.

Jesuit Missionary, 1851.

However, the writer of Source 5 was tricked. The Treaty was a sham: the government had no real intention of honouring it. The results were to be extreme, as we shall see later on in this book, as its failure was to set the scene for the devastating Plains Wars.

---

1. What was the belief among most white Americans about Indians?

2. a) What was the 'Frontier'? Use Source 1 to help you.

   b) What was the effect of disease on Indians?

   c) Why did the Oregon Trail worsen relations?

   d) What was the effect of discovering gold?

3. Use Source 4 to describe the Fort Laramie Treaty.

---

4. a) What changes do Sources 2 and 3 show in the relations between Indians and whites?

   b) Does Source 5 show a change for the better?

5. 'By 1851 relations between whites and Indians had changed for the worse.' How far do you agree with this statement?

A HOSTILE ENVIRONMENT

Homesteaders – or 'sodbusters' as they were often called – faced a life of hard work for which they were often poorly prepared. Many intended using Eastern farming methods which would not work in the climate of the West. Through trial and error the sodbusters developed a system of successful farming that changed the face of the Prairies, but often at great personal expense. Even by the end of our period conditions could be appalling.

SOURCE 1

Most frontier farmers . . . had very little machinery or livestock, and they farmed only a few acres. They produced part of their own living by growing potatoes and other vegetables, wheat and flour, and by raising livestock for meat. But they were by no means self-sufficient . . . other supplies were obtained with money obtained from selling butter, a few bushels of grain, or an occasional hog or calf.

Gilbert C. Fite, The Farmers' Frontier, *1966.*

SOURCE 2

I take my pen in hand to let you know that we are starving to death. It is pretty hard to do without anything to eat here in this God-forsaken country . . . I haven't had nothing to eat today and it is 3 o'clock.

Letter to the Governor of Kansas, 1894.

Why were conditions so bad? The Prairies have extremes of weather – as we have already seen – with potentially disastrous effects. Drought devastated crops and left people hungry: between June 1859 and November 1860 in some areas no good rain fell at all. During severe winters thousands of animals died. In 1885 there was a severe winter: some cowboys froze to death trying to save their animals. The next summer was one of drought followed by snows starting in October, leading to an unspeakably severe winter. In February 1887 one local newspaper reported that 40% of all livestock had been killed during the winter.

The following sources will help you piece together some of the problems people faced in their hostile environment.

SOURCE 3

When the thunder jarred the earth and electric balls of fire split the wind-lashed sheets of rain, a nervous herd of longhorns was most apt to suddenly explode and go thundering away in any direction.

Harold McCracken, The American Cowboy, *1973.*

SOURCE 4

Dust storm hits the town of Springfield, Colorado.

SOURCE 5

We were all playing in our shirt sleeves, without hats or mittens. Suddenly we looked up and saw something coming rolling towards us with great fury . . . and making a loud noise. It looked like a long string of big bales of cotton, each one bound tightly with heavy cords of silver.

O. W. Coursey.

SOURCE 6

The weather was terribly hot. At the end of the second day cattle commenced to grind their teeth in their suffering . . . At night these groans and grinding of their teeth was the most horrible thing I have ever went through.

Bob Fudge, c.1930.

SOURCE 7

Painting entitled 'The Hard Winter' by W. Koerner, 1932.

SOURCE 8

Nothing escaped their appetite. They consumed crops, prairie grass, the leaves and bark of trees, leather boots and harness straps, even fence posts, door frames and the sweat-stained wooden handles of axes and ploughs.

A more unusual calamity happened in the 1870s (especially in 1874) when plagues of grasshoppers caused massive destruction. From H. Horn, The Pioneers, *1974.*

The most feared human danger came from Indian attacks. Although these were far less common than people believed, they were an ever-present threat. The horrors of what could happen chilled the blood of homesteaders.

SOURCE 9

Her head, arms and face (were) full of bruises and sores, and her nose actually burnt off to the bone – all the fleshy end gone, and a great scab formed on the end of the bone. Both nostrils were wide open and without flesh. She told a piteous tale of how dreadfully the Indians had beaten her, and how they would wake her up from sleep by sticking a chunk of fire to her flesh, especially to her nose, and how they would shout and laugh like fiends when she cried.

Mary A. Maverick, Memoirs, *1921 (about an event in 1840).*

1. What was farming like according to Sources 1 and 2?

2. Why were these such bad times:
   a) June 1859 to November 1860;
   b) 1874;
   c) the winter of 1886–87?

3. Copy out and fill in using Sources 3 to 9. Use your own knowledge and understanding to complete this.

Problem	Effects

4. a) What do you think homesteaders thought about their conditions?
   b) Do you think opinions would change after several years?

5. Why do you think homesteaders wanted to bring up children in such a hostile environment?

41

NEW TECHNOLOGY AND METHODS

Technology and new methods can result in both change and progress. Our modern society has witnessed many of these: from home computers to digital world communications. Used properly they can make life both easier and better. In the American West of the late 19th century, people used the ideas and technologies that had begun in Britain with the Industrial, Agricultural and Transport revolutions. This unit uses pictorial and diagrammatic evidence for you to examine what was achieved in a very short time.

SOURCE 1

Artist's impression of Great Wheat Fields, Dakota, 1878.

SOURCE 2

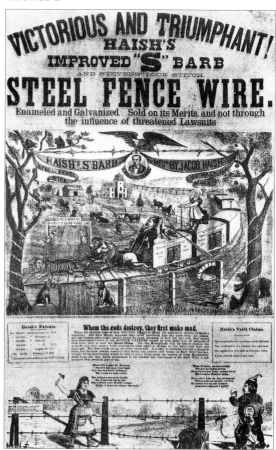

Advert for barbed wire which led to the end of open field ranching.

SOURCE 3

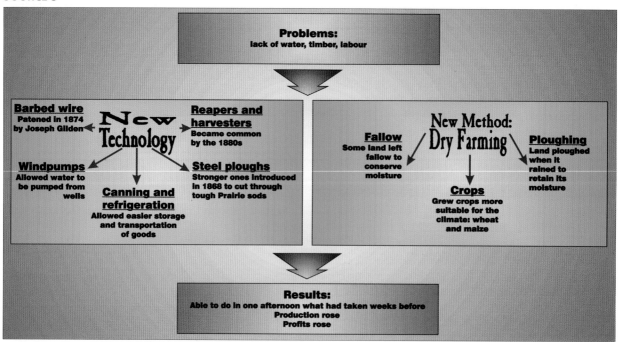

Problems:
lack of water, timber, labour

New Technology

Barbed wire
Patened in 1874 by Joseph Gilden

Reapers and harvesters
Became common by the 1880s

Windpumps
Allowed water to be pumped from wells

Canning and refrigeration
Allowed easier storage and transportation of goods

Steel ploughs
Stronger ones introduced in 1868 to cut through tough Prairie sods

New Method: Dry Farming

Fallow
Some land left fallow to conserve moisture

Ploughing
Land ploughed when it rained to retain its moisture

Crops
Grew crops more suitable for the climate: wheat and maize

Results:
Able to do in one afternoon what had taken weeks before
Production rose
Profits rose

SOURCE 4

A harvester from around 1885.

SOURCE 6

A windpump from the 1880s.

SOURCE 5

A steam tractor from 1890.

1. Study Source 3.
   a) What problems did homesteaders face?
   b) What new technologies were introduced?
   c) Explain what Dry Farming was.
   d) What were the results of these changes?

2. Source 1 is an artist's impression. Is this more useful than Source 6 in finding out about new technology?

3. Why are advertisements (Source 2) useful to historians?

4. Study Sources 4 and 5. What are the
   a) advantages, b) disadvantages of using these as evidence?

5. Is the diagram (Source 3) more or less useful than text to find out about this topic?

6. 'Pictorial evidence is a poor substitute for a good piece of writing.' Do you agree?

WHOSE LAND?

SOURCE 1

'Buffalo on the Plains', a painting by Albert Bierstadt.

Source 1 shows a beautiful landscape in Upper Missouri with herds of buffalo running free: it was painted by a white American but captured perfectly the Native American landscape – open, free and without fences. Indians believed that the earth not only belonged to all people, but to the animals and plants too, and that it needed to be respected. Of particular importance were their tribal lands. The Indians in Source 2 sum up typical attitudes.

SOURCE 2

A) The soil you see is not ordinary land – it is the dust of the blood, the flesh, and the bones of our ancestors . . . The land, as it is, is my blood and my dead; it is holy.

Crow Indian.

B) The great chief [the US president] sends word that he wishes to buy our land . . . How can you buy or sell the sky, the warmth of the land? The idea is strange to us. If we do not own the freshness of the air and the sparkle of the water, how can you buy them?

Chief Sealth to the US President, 1854.

White Americans had a very different view about land, believing that all land could be owned: this was to be a major area of conflict with Indians. No sooner had European colonies begun in the early 17th century, than fences were built to symbolise land ownership. By 1840 this issue affected more white Americans, as expansion westwards was seen as not only necessary but as a natural right. This idea was called 'Manifest Destiny', as the historian in Source 3 explains. This

SOURCE 5

Painting called 'Manifest Destiny' by John Gast, 1872.

B) This occupation of wild territory . . . is at this moment sweeping onward to the Pacific with accelerated activity and force . . . pushed onward by the hand of God . . . Fronting the Union on every side is a vast army of pioneer . . . from every village, county, city, and State in the Union, and by emigrants from other nations . . .

North America will . . . expand and fit itself to the continent; to control the oceans on either hand, and eventually the continents beyond.

William Gilpin, 1858.

C) We have not yet fulfilled our destiny. New territory is spread out for us to subdue and fertilise; new races are presented for us to civilise, educate and absorb; new triumphs for us to achieve for the cause of freedom.

Daniel Dickinson, 1848.

ideology (belief) was used to justify forcing Indians off their ancient lands, and to allow the white occupation of the American West, as Sources 4 and 5 illustrate.

Despite Manifest Destiny's grand ideas, many Americans did not support it, including most of the government. Most Americans saw issues in terms of what affected them locally: they were more concerned with getting their own small parcels of land rather than worrying about a 'God-given' scheme for the whole continent.

SOURCE 3

It meant expansion, granted by Heaven . . . In some minds it meant expansion over the region to the Pacific; in others, over the North American Continent; in others, over the hemisphere . . . it attracted enough people by the mid 1840s to become a movement . . . It meant opportunity for neighbouring peoples to gain admission to the American Union.

Frederick Merk, Manifest Destiny, *1963.*

SOURCE 4

A) North America was only inhabited by wandering tribes, who took no thought of the natural riches of the soil, and that vast country was still, properly speaking, an empty continent, a desert land awaiting its inhabitants . . .

Civilised Europeans are peacefully spreading over those fertile plains . . . Three or four thousand soldiers . . . make ready the procession of civilisation across the waste . . . The time will . . . come when one hundred and fifty millions of men will be living in North America, all equals, one race, owing their origin to the same cause, and preserving the same civilisation, the same language, the same religion, the same habits, and the same manners.

Alexis de Tocqueville, 1831.

---

1. What was the Native American attitude towards land?

2. a) What was 'Manifest Destiny'?

b) When did it become a movement?

c) Why was this movement bad for Indians?

d) How popular was it?

---

3. In what ways do Sources 1 and 5 show conflicting attitudes towards land ownership?

4. What evidence is there that Manifest Destiny was:

a) racist;

b) huge in its scope;

c) offering freedom;

d) God's intention?

HOMES

Plains Indians

As we have seen, Plains Indians lived a nomadic life which meant that their homes had to be portable. The result was a simple but extremely effective design: the tipi. The tipi was built from a circle of long poles tied at the top over packed down earth. The walls were made up of easily available buffalo cows' skins sewn together with buffalo sinew in a half-moon shape. The tipi covering was painted with different pictures and patterns according to the particular tribe. A small tipi took 11 cowhides whilst a big lodge might require as many as 21. Inside the tipi benches were made from sods covered with bundles of grass that formed the foundations for benches during the day and beds at night. It was about 4.5m in diameter. At the centre of the tipi was a fire with smoke escaping through the top vent: unfortunately this did not always work and tipis got filled with smoke making them unpleasant. Some other tribes built different homes, such as the Mandans' lodges (see pages 8–9).

Tipis were very versatile, as George Catlin tells us:

SOURCE 1

These lodges, or tents, are taken down in a few minutes by the squaws, when they wish to change their location, and easily transported to any part of the country where they wish to encamp; and they generally move some six or eight times in the course of the summer; following the immense herds of buffaloes, as they range over these vast plains.

George Catlin, 1844.

SOURCE 2

Catlin's painting of a Comanche chief's children in front of their tipi, 1834.

Homesteaders

White homesteaders soon learned that their homes needed to suit the environment and be made out of locally available materials too. For those who made the journey to the West, setting up home was far from easy. You will now see life through the eyes of Howard Ruede who wrote these accounts between 1877 and 1878. Use these extracts to piece together what homesteaders' homes were like.

SOURCE 3

Sod . . . is the only material the homesteader has at hand, unless he happens to be one of the fortunates who secured a creek claim with timber suitable for house logs . . .

The sod is about 2 feet [0.6m] thick at the ground, and slopes off on the top . . . The roof is composed of a ridge pole and rafters of rough split logs, on which is laid corn stalks, and on top of those are two layers of sod. The roof has a very straight pitch, for if it had more, the sod would wash off when there is a heavy rain . . .

At first these sod houses are unplastered, and this is thought perfectly all right, but such a house is somewhat cold in the winter, as the crevices between the sods admit some cold air. Plaster is very good unless it happens to get wet . . . Some sod houses are mighty comfortable places to go in cold weather, and it don't take much fire to keep them warm.

The people who live in sod houses . . . are pestered with swarms of bed bugs . . . The bugs infest . . . in countless thousands . . . Where the sod houses are plastered the bed bugs are not such a nuisance . . . Fleas . . . are natives too and do their best to drive out the intruding settlers. Just have a dirt floor and you have fleas, sure . . . Coal oil and water are sometimes used to sprinkle the floor, but that holds back the pest only for a short time . . . People who have board floors are not bothered so much with these fleas.

Howard Ruede, 1878.

SOURCE 4

A sod house. Dirt often showered in from the ceiling. Its damp and soggy roof threatened to cave in, and it leaked relentlessly in wet weather.

SOURCE 5

A dug-out cut into the side of a hill. These were inhabited by the poorest people and were unpleasant, damp dwellings.

1. a) Use Source 2 to make a diagram of a tipi. Label: door flap; smoke flap; smoke flap pole; wooden poles; buffalo covering; designs.

   b) Write an explanation to accompany the diagram.

2. a) What was a sod house?

   b) Why did people have to live in these?

   c) What was wrong with them?

3. a) How useful is the account of a homesteader like Ruede in finding out about life on the Prairies?

   b) What would a historian have to do to find out more about settlers' living conditions?

4. 'The tipi and the sod house are both excellent examples showing people responding to their local environment.' How far do you agree with this statement?

HOMELIFE

Homelife for Plains Indians developed over centuries and was male-dominated. Sometimes men could be very cruel towards their women: the common penalty for female adultery was having the nose cut off by the husband. Polygamy (having several wives) was common: this was quite sensible as there were far more females than males due to the high death rates for males in war. Homelife was very ordered indeed, with clear expectations governing behaviour. Girls played with toy tipis and deerskin dolls, whilst boys played with toy bows and arrows. An example of how carefully behaviour was worked out is shown in Source 1.

SOURCE 1

Visitors to a tipi.

- If the door is open then enter. If it is closed, wait to be invited in.
- A male visitor goes to the right and waits to be invited to sit in the guest place. The woman follows the man and goes to the right.
- At a feast guests bring their own bowls and spoons.
- No visitor should pass between the fire and another person.
- Women must not sit crossed-legged like men.
- In male-only company the younger men should only speak if invited to do so by their elders.
- When the host cleans his pipe everyone should leave.

SOURCE 2

Source 2 shows a family scene in a tipi. Much work fell on the women with a large part of this taken up with cooking. Buffalo provided the staple diet. Women also collected the vegetables needed, and in some tribes learnt farming skills. Native American eating could be very different from western ideas (Source 3).

SOURCE 3

I had observed a litter of well-grown black puppies . . . Seizing one of them by the hind paw, she dragged him out . . . hammered him on the head till she killed him . . . The squaw, holding the puppy by the legs, swung him to and fro through the blaze of a fire, until the hair was singed off . . . She unsheathed her knife and cut him into small pieces, which she dropped into a kettle to boil . . . A dog-feast is the greatest compliment a Dahcotah can offer to his guest.

Francis Parkman, The Oregon Trail, *1847.*

Unlike the Plains Indians, settlers' lifestyles were new as they came to grips with their harsh environment. Commentators both then and now stress how hard people's homelives were.

SOURCE 4

There was an almost constant struggle to get enough money to buy the bare necessities of life. This was especially true in the early years of settlement.

Gilbert C. Fite, The American Destiny: The Age of the West, *1976.*

Inside a tipi.

Everyday life in their sod house could be bleak, with none of the comforts we expect today. The extracts in Source 5 give a feeling of what life was like. However, communities developed, trying to make the most of their lives and encouraging people to enjoy themselves wherever possible. Fairs, dances and other activities were arranged, especially important for young single people to meet. Towns developed, bringing with them shops, schools and other facilities: one historian discovered that some people went into town – 15 km away – up to three times a week during the autumn and winter.

SOURCE 5

A) We haven't had any washing done yet, because we have nothing to our credit . . . Underclothes I don't wear . . . and socks there are none to wash, as they also have been discarded.

Howard Ruede, 1877.

B) For breakfast we had corn bread, salt pork and black coffee. For dinner, greens, wild ones at that, boiled pork, and cold corn bread washed down with 'beverage' (which) was vinegar and brown sugar and warm creek water.

Mollie Sanford, c.1880.

C) It is comical to see how gingerly our wives handled these chips at first. They commenced by picking them up between two sticks . . . Soon they used a rag and then a corner of their apron . . . Now it is out of the bread, into the chips and back again – and not even a dust of the hands.

Kansas newspaper editor, 1877. Cow chips were dried cow pats which were burnt for fuel.

SOURCE 6

This photograph shows Nebraska prairie sod being peeled off by homesteaders in rows and cut into blocks. This was used to build sod houses.

1. What are the main features in Sources 1 and 2?
2. What do Sources 4 and 5 say about settlers' conditions?

3. To what extent was Indian society male-dominated?
4. Why did homesteaders go west when life was so difficult?
5. 'Homelife was far tougher for homesteaders than Indians.' Do you agree?

WOMEN

Plains women

As we saw in the last chapter, Indian squaws (women) played a secondary role to men and were usually relegated to the menial tasks. A recent historian pointed out that in some tribes a few women were listened to in the council, but then said that in other cases a woman was 'worth something between a horse and a dog'. Source 1 shows a pathetic-looking squaw collecting wood for her family in appalling weather. George Catlin describes their position in Source 2.

SOURCE 1

Hidatsa woman collecting firewood, Upper Missouri.

SOURCE 2

Women . . . are always held in a rank inferior to that of the men, in relation to whom in many respects they stand rather in the light of menials and slaves than otherwise . . . It becomes a matter of necessity for a chief to have in his wigwam a sufficient number of such handmaids or menials to perform numerous duties and drudgeries . . . and give to his lodge the appearance of respectability which is not ordinarily seen.

George Catlin, 1844.

Although warfare was considered the domain of men, squaws defended their camp when the men went on a raiding party. Some accompanied a war party as cooks or to hold horses. There are even a very few recorded instances of female warriors! However, a squaw was seen as the home-maker often doing very strenuous jobs; and if she was not doing domestic work, she was most likely preparing buffalo hides and drying meat. This began after a hunt with the hides pegged out, and meat, fat and membranes scrapped away. Tanning was done using a mixture of liver, fat, and brains: this process usually took six days for one hide! Hides were usually decorated which gave squaws the opportunity to display their artistic skills. They were highly praised for this, especially quilling with bird or porcupine quills that had been boiled to make them supple and then stained different colours. These skills also allowed squaws to take pride in their own appearance as Catlin describes in Source 3.

SOURCE 3

The women in all these upper and western tribes are decently dressed, and many of them with great beauty and taste; their dresses are all of deer or goat skins, extending from their chins quite down to the feet. These dresses are in many instances trimmed with ermine, and ornamented with porcupine quills and beads with exceeding ingenuity.

George Catlin, 1844.

A squaw often found herself married to a man with several other wives. If he died she was expected to mourn by cutting her arms with a knife and pulling hair out. In some tribes she would be found a new husband after the mourning period had ended.

---

1. a) In what ways was life tough for Plains squaws?

b) What important jobs did they do?

c) What does Source 3 tell us about their appearance?

---

2. How accurate a reflection is Source 1 of Indian life for squaws on the basis of your study?

3. Why did women accept their low status?

SOURCE 4

'The Madonna of the Prairies', a painting by W. Koerner.

'Westering women'

The condition of white settlers was both different and similar. Source 4 shows a traditional view of a woman settler. This 19th-century saint-like woman – complete with halo effect – in fact had to face a harsh life once she arrived in the West, as Source 5 graphically illustrates.

SOURCE 5

Still I must sweep, and churn and brew,
And make my dresses nice to view;
And nurse the baby, read the news,
Darn socks, keep buttons on the shoes,
Play the piano, beat the steak,
Then last, not least, this undertake . . .
If men to such a task were set,
They's lock their door, and swear and fret . . .
But we must learn a hundred trades
Without apprenticeship or aids,
And practice all with equal skill,
'Tis their good pleasure, our good will.

Texas poetess.

The part played by white women in the development of the American West was far more important than many would have us believe. Here are two modern interpretations that attack the traditional view.

SOURCE 6

A) Perhaps no image in American history and literature is more deeply embedded in the American mind than that of the frightened, tearful woman wrenched from home and hearth and dragged off into the terrible West where she is condemned to a life of lonely terror among savage beasts and preying Indians. Overworked and overbirthed, she lived through a long succession of dreary days of toil and loneliness until . . . she resigned herself to a hard life and early death. This tragic figure appeared so often in American literature that she assumed almost legendary status . . . Unfortunately, these literary stereotypes have found their way into historical portraits of frontier women . . . Pioneering women were neither the sunbonnet saints of traditional literature nor the exploited drudges of the new feminist studies. Women's lives . . . varied with the circumstances of their backgrounds, family, [and] education.

Sandra Myres, Westering Women, *1982.*

B) There seems to be a popular notion that women of the old West were either prostitutes or wives or mothers. In truth, women played a great variety of roles, according to their needs and the needs of their families. In the often harsh environment of the West, rules were set aside in favour of practicality more often than not.

Virginia Hopkins, Pioneers of the Old West, *1988.*

Conditions dictated that the traditional Victorian ideas of women had to be scrapped in favour of something more practical. Thus women played an active part in all aspects of homelife, including those traditionally thought to be 'men's work': building the house; and working the land, even extended to the strenuous task of ploughing. Within the house the woman kept the 'soddie' bearable. She draped muslin across the ceiling in the summer to stop bugs getting in, and might often be seen cooking with rain pouring in. She had to take responsibility for the family's health at a time when available medicines were almost non-existent. They used turpentine to clean wounds, and chicken meat to suck out snake bites. Women sometimes had to give birth on their own, or with only their children to help them. Even with all of their skills, however, infant mortality was high: 25%–30% of all children born died within a year. Measles and the flu killed thousands of children.

Modern historians have highlighted this role for women (Source 6). Women played a vital role in taming the West. Initially they were in a tiny minority. When a family arrived with teenage daughters the behaviour and dress of local men improved considerably! Women played the vital role in educating children at a time when men did not consider teaching proper men's work. Women also helped bring religion to the West, and played a vital role in setting up churches and persuading their men to attend. They also campaigned for curbs on alcohol that was wrecking many families, persuading Kansas to introduce prohibition [banning alcohol] in 1860.

Important work was carried on in the struggle for women to get equality and the vote. The first women got union recognition in the cigar-making union in 1867, with the Working Women's Association agitating for more rights elsewhere. As a result of a great deal of

work, Wyoming became the first state to grant women the vote in 1869, partly because they were few and hence did not pose a threat to men. Utah gave women the vote in 1870. By 1900, however, only five states had granted women the vote.

It was possible for women to be independent and earn a living in their own right. The obvious professions – which past historians have concentrated on – were working in music halls, or as prostitutes. In San Francisco alone it is estimated that there were 10,000 prostitutes in the 1880s! Some women became camp followers, following mining, railroad and army camps and providing a full range of services for the men! Some women, however, were successful in business: this

SOURCE 7

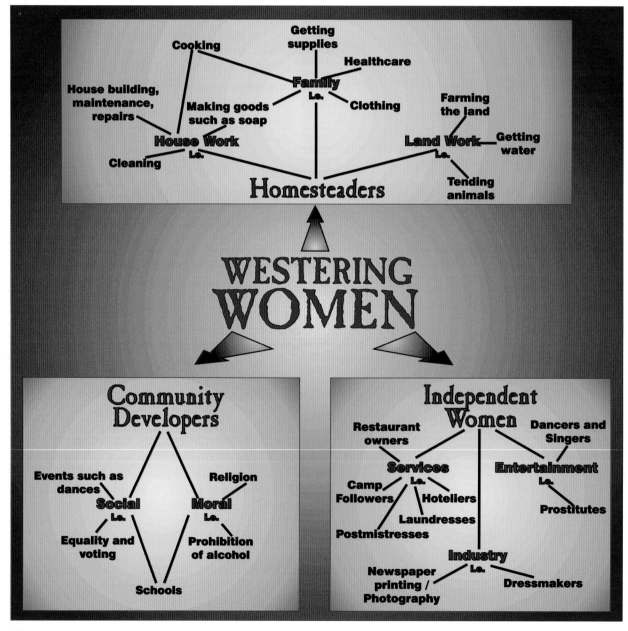

SOURCE 8

Becker sisters on their ranch, San Luis Valley, 1884.

ranged from running hotels, to operating photographic companies. One woman made $10,000 washing clothes! Another, a black woman called Sallie Frazier, ran a thriving restaurant in Dodge City and managed to deal with Dodge's difficult male customers!

Source 8 shows women ranchers branding a calf: several women became successful ranchers and owned farms. Some women even turned to crime, such as Jennie Metcalf who was involved in rustling horses, highway robbery, and even bank robbery!

4. a) According to Source 6, what was the traditional role of women?

b) How does this source criticise this?

5. Study Source 6. Use this plus the text and Source 7 to write an account of the role of women under these headings:

a) homesteaders;

b) community life;

c) independent women.

6. Sources 4 and 5 present an incomplete impression of 'westering women'. Does this mean these are of no use to historians?

7. Study Sources 4 and 7. Which is the most useful for historians in studying the American West?

8. Why is it important to consider new interpretations of women's roles when trying to understand the American West?

9. In what ways was life for Plains women and 'westering women' similar and different?

SPIRITS AND THE SUN DANCE

Imagine a small number of white Americans like George Catlin in the 1830s and Francis Parkman in the 1840s exploring the lands of Native Americans: what a strange world they must have seen. As God-fearing men, nothing could have prepared them for the world of Indian religion which both intrigued and shocked.

Travellers were told stories of how people began:

SOURCE 1

Inktomi took some dirt and from it made a man and a woman. The new people asked Inktomi what they should eat. Inktomi did not want people to eat his animal friends, so he created buffalo. He told the people that they should eat the buffalo.

Indian Creation myth.

They were told that there were three worlds:

- under the lake on which the earth floated were powerful underworld spirits controlling plants and animals;
- above the earth beyond the sky was the upper world with spirits that matched those of the underworld;
- on earth there were the spirits of the four winds changing the seasons.

They would find that different tribes had different versions of this basic belief. When they asked about God they would be told of the Great Spirit some tribes called Wankantanka.

Travellers were intrigued by the Medicine Man who had extraordinary powers to communicate with the spirits all around them: some would claim the power to cure illness or see the future. George Catlin made several studies of these men: Source 2 is an example.

Francis Parkman got an insight into another side of their religious devotion when he inspected an Indian:

SOURCE 3

Each of his arms was marked as if deeply gashed with a knife at regular intervals, and there were other scars also, of a different character, on his back and on either breast.

SOURCE 2

Old Bear, a medicine man. Painting by George Catlin, 1832.

They were the traces of the tortures which these Indians . . . inflict upon themselves at certain seasons. In part, it may be to gain the glory of courage and endurance, but chiefly as an act of self-sacrifice to secure the favour of the spirits.

Francis Parkman.

Parkman may have had some knowledge of this custom from earlier travellers such as Catlin (Source 4).

SOURCE 4

I entered the medicine-house as I would have entered a church, and expected to see something extraordinary and strange in the form of worship or devotion. But alas, little did I expect to see the interior of their holy temple turned into a slaughter-house, and its floor strewed with the blood of its fanatic devotees. Little did I think that I was entering a house of God, where His blinded worshippers were to pollute its sacred interior with their blood, suffering and tortures.

George Catlin, 1830s.

'The Cutting Scene', a painting after George Catlin.

The Sun Dance

Only very few white Americans were able to see one of the Indians' most sacred ceremonies: the Sun Dance. This took place for about a week in the summer or early autumn to ensure that the buffalo continued to run and crops grow. Tipis were placed in a circle with a dancing area in the middle. In the Cheyenne version they built a New Life lodge to house the main ceremony with a large central post placed at the centre, in front of which men danced on tiptoes for several days. The main focus of the ritual were the acts of individual self-torture. Men had skewers placed into their chests with ropes attaching them to the central post. They danced, pulling against the ropes until their skin ripped free. In extreme cases the skewers were placed under the eyes. George Catlin witnessed several of these ceremonies which filled him with horror. Source 5 is a copy of his painting 'The Cutting Scene' showing a Mandan variation of this ceremony. In this version the men were spun around before fainting. Once they were cut free, they crawled to the masked man in the right corner who cut off one or two of their fingers.

1. What were the three worlds Indians believed in?
2. What powers had the Medicine Men?
3. What do Sources 3 and 4 tell us about their religion?
4. Write a description to explain what is happening in Source 5.

5. People knew how painful these ceremonies were. Why did they participate?
6. The Medicine Man in Source 2 would oversee these ceremonies to please the Sun and Great Spirit. Did this make him a cruel man?
7. Does this help prove that Indians were barbaric and savage?

DESERT SAINTS

Religion was very important in the West. Many communities did not even have a church: people went to private houses for 'meetings', including people of all denominations who listened to a preacher from whatever faith was available! Meetings proved very popular and were usually full and often over-flowing. As towns and cities became established separate churches grew up. For most people, these existing Christian religions served their needs. However, amid this, an entirely American faith developed, far more radical and controversial than any of the faiths that had travelled from Europe to America: The Church of Jesus Christ of the Latter-day Saints – commonly called the Mormons.

Part 1 : the golden plates

The Mormons have a remarkable tale to tell. In 1820 a teenager, Joseph Smith, said that he had seen a vision of God the Father, his son Jesus Christ, and an angel called Moroni. The angel told Smith about a set of golden plates containing religious writings. He found the plates in 1823, but was not able to study them until 1827 when he was 21. The holy writings told of a band of Hebrews who fled the Holy Land in 600 BC and were able to find America. In America they divided into the Nephites and Lamanites and built wonderful cities. The scene moved forward hundreds of years to the crucifixion of Christ in the Holy Land. According to these writings, Christ came to visit them in America.

SOURCE 6

'Saints driven from Jackson County, Missouri', a painting by C. C. A. Christensen.

The people lived in peace after this, until a terrible war broke out and around AD 421 the Lamanites destroyed the Nephites. The Lamanites had mixed with groups from Europe and Asia and become the ancestors of the Native Americans. Moroni and his father Mormon of the Nephites survived and made the plates.

Part 2 : the search for Zion

This amazing story formed the basis of the Book of Mormon and the central belief of the Mormons. Smith set up the church in 1830, with its members calling themselves 'Latter-Day Saints'. By 1831 they had settled in Kirtland, Ohio, where they built their first temple. However, they soon ran into trouble: their beliefs were unacceptable to most Americans at that time and soon vicious persecution began. Smith was tarred and feathered in 1832. Source 6 shows attacks on Mormons in 1833. Many people lost money in a bank that Smith had set in Kirtland which failed in 1837. This was the last straw and the Mormons had to flee for their lives. Each time they tried to settle somewhere local people hounded them out. Hopes that they could build a new 'Zion' or City of God in Independence, Missouri were also dashed. Rumours spread that the Mormons intended joining with Indians to conquer Missouri: the Governor said they should be exterminated, or made to leave the State.

The following year they moved to Illinois and built the town of Nauvoo: at long last it seemed that they would be able to live in peace and practise their faith. Nauvoo soon became a city of 8,000 people as recruits flocked to join the Mormons, including many from Britain. The Mormons still feared persecution and formed a militia for their protection. Controversy surrounded Smith, who was suspected of counterfeiting and theft. Then rumours started that Smith was to stand as a Presidential candidate. More shocking than this was the discovery that the Mormons had begun to practise polygamy. This revelation was too much for the gentiles (non-Mormons). When Smith and his brother were jailed in 1844 a furious mob stormed the jail and murdered both of them.

Part 3 : exodus to Salt Lake City

Smith's death and the issue of polygamy led to splits in the movement. The majority accepted Brigham Young as their leader (Source 7): he led the Mormons until his death in 1877. By 1846 the group was on the move again in search of sanctuary. Young decided that a new site had to be remote: somewhere no-one else would want to go, and outside the control of the US government. He eventually chose the Great Salt Lake area as it was barren, but had mountain streams nearby that could be used for irrigation. It was also controlled by Mexico. Young would not be put off by those who strongly advised against this location: he said that if there was a place on earth that no-one else wanted then this was the place for the Mormons.

The journey to Salt Lake is a tale of bravery and utter determination. Source 8 shows the settlers 2,250km journey. It was a mammoth undertaking – to move 15,000 people, of all ages – requiring military precision. Nevertheless, the journey was appalling and many hundreds of people died on it. Many of the settlers were inadequately prepared for the difficulties of the journey or for the terrible weather they encountered.

SOURCE 7

Brigham Young, from a Mormon poster.

SOURCE 8

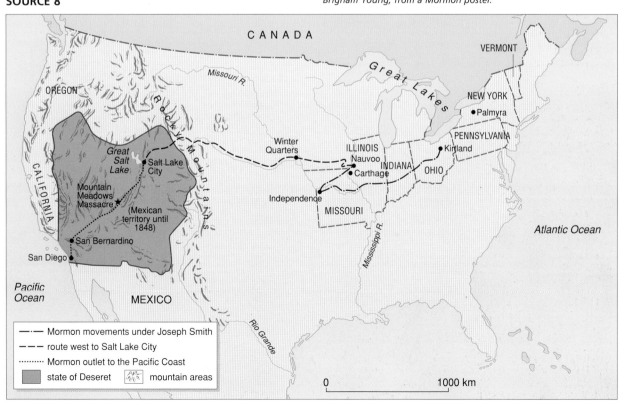

The route of the Mormons westwards.

57

Part 4 : making the desert bloom

The first party arrived at Salt Lake in 1847. Within three months Salt Lake was home to nearly 2,000 people. The settlers had begun a building programme; set up a government; and had begun to organise trade. The Mormons kept their own militia and officers were often members of the priesthood. To 'make the desert bloom' the Mormons invested a great deal of energy in a complex irrigation system. However, the settlers soon found that only a small portion of the land could be irrigated, and much required alternative techniques. Young decided that there was to be no private ownership of land or the water supply. To create a fair system, everyone would be allocated what they needed. Early success was undermined by disaster: insects and other animals ate crops, and livestock was stolen by Indians or killed by wolves. By the spring of 1848 the new settlers were starving and were forced to eat tree bark and thistle tops. Despite this, converts kept flocking to the new settlement. Fortunately the harvest was better in this year.

The development of Salt Lake City progressed, with elaborate plans to build a temple at its centre. The huge temple was begun in 1851 and took 40 years to complete (Source 9). At the same time the Mormons set about making themselves self-sufficient. This needed a large influx of people so an extensive recruitment campaign was started. The need for more people was believed to be one of the reasons behind polygamy that was practised by 10%–20% of Mormons: Brigham Young had 27 wives and 57 children by 16 of them, though this was not typical. Source 10 shows an anti-Mormon cartoon with Young hiding on the wardrobe whilst his two new brides are attacked by his other wives! One Mormon historian found that all leaders of the movement practised polygamy: this may also have made it very difficult for them to leave the movement. Polygamy was also a major obstacle to their acceptance in America, especially after it was openly acknowledged by the church in 1852.

Unlike many other emigrants to the West the Mormons supported the Indians who, as we have seen, they believed to be the descendants of an ancient Hebrew

SOURCE 9

The Mormon Temple at Salt Lake City, Utah.

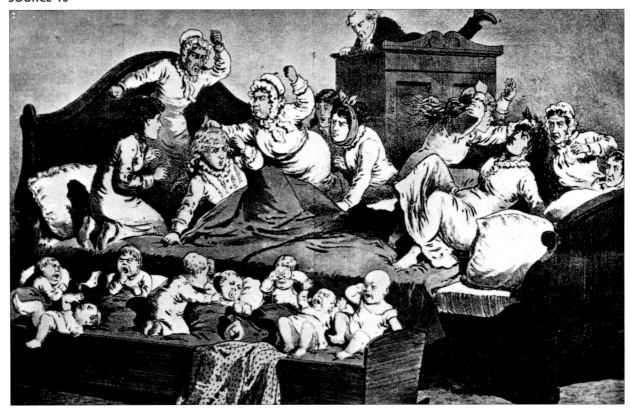

Anti-Mormon cartoon of Brigham Young and his wives.

tribe. Young instructed his people to be kind to them and organisations were set up to help feed and clothe them. This worsened relations with the US Government who suspected the Mormons of plotting with the Indians.

Part 5 : the struggle for Deseret

Young's main aims were for the Mormons to be self-sufficient and to govern themselves. These objectives were dealt a severe blow when the USA took control of the territory from Mexico in 1848. In 1849 Young sought admission to the Union with the intention of calling the state Deseret (land of the honey-bee): the application was turned down. In 1850 the territory was named Utah (after the Ute Indians) with Young as its Governor. US officials frequently clashed with the Mormons in a struggle for control. Matters came to a head in 1857 when a non-Mormon was imposed as Governor with 2,500 troops to bring the area under tighter US control. Later that year 140 settlers from Missouri were massacred at Mountain Meadows. The blame for the massacre fell on the Mormons who in turn blamed the Indians.

In an attempt not to escalate the situation, the Government sent a 'peace commission' to Utah in the spring of 1858. They negotiated with the Mormons to end the so-called 'Mormon War'. However, the US government refused to allow Utah to become a state until polygamy was renounced by the church. The Mormons banned polygamy in 1890, and Utah was finally accepted into the Union in 1896.

1. Use the information in this unit to create a timeline showing the history of the Mormons in the 19th century.

2. Unlike the other units in this book, this is an historical narrative without any written sources included.

   a) What types of written (i) primary and (ii) secondary evidence could be used to research more on this topic?

   b) 'Studying the Mormons using an historical narrative is much better than working through sources to discover their history yourself.' Do you agree?

3. 'The Mormons brought all of the trouble they encountered on themselves.' Discuss this statement as a short essay.

GROWTH OF THE AMERICAN WEST

The vast development of the American West is one of the most amazing phases of history. Several million people travelled west to begin new lives during this time. The stunning effect of this is summed up in these contemporary accounts (Source 1).

SOURCE 1

A) The movement of settlers . . . had now become an exodus, a stampede. Hardly anything else was talked about as neighbours met one another on the road . . . Every man who could sell out had gone west or was going . . . Farmer after farmer joined the march to Kansas, Nebraska, and Dakota . . . All around me . . . the talk was all of land, land! . . . Each voice was aquiver with hope, each eye alight with anticipation of certain success.

Hamlin Garland, A Son of the Middle Border, *1925.*

B) Imagination can scarcely keep pace with the increase of the western country . . . Villages, towns, populous cities have sprung up as by magic.

Land Commissioner's Report, 1851.

We can get a better idea of this by looking at official government statistics (Source 2). Unfortunately there are no official figures before 1850, and for some territories, these do not begin until later. The graphs show the massive increase in population: Washington went from only 1,200 people in 1850, to a staggering 357,230 40 years later; whilst Arizona more than doubled its population between 1880 and 1890. The statistics for California and Texas are shown in a separate graph as numbers are too high to allow them on the main graph: you can see this by the inclusion of Utah on both graphs to allow you to compare them. Source 3 shows the growing Virginia City at this time. This increase was possible due to the improvement in communications – such as the railroads – and because of the Homestead Act of 1862 (see pages 22–23). Texas was particularly important as it joined the USA after the War with Mexico.

Immigrants, mainly from Europe, made up a large part of this growth, although there were many Chinese too. In the year 1879–80 450,000 immigrants arrived, occupying 7,000,000 acres of land. This was nothing compared to the highest number of 800,000 in 1882.

As these territories grew, so the government responded. All public land had to be surveyed and split up into townships. The Government organised all of this land into territories. The next stage was for these territories to become states as part of the Union. Source 4 shows the slow development of these: some such as Arizona were not incorporated into the Union until the early 20th century.

SOURCE 2

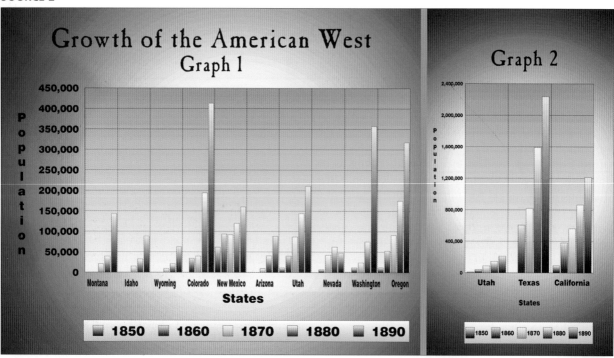

SOURCE 4

The states of the USA and their admission into the Union.

SOURCE 3

A new town: Virginia City, Nevada, 1860s.

1. What impression does Source 1 give of the growth of the American West?

2. a) How did California and Texas grow during this period?

   b) Choose three other territories from Source 2. Describe their growth.

   c) Which territory shows the most dramatic growth?

3. How many immigrants arrived in the early 1880s?

4. Use Source 4 to make a table of states joining the Union after the original states. Use the key for your headings.

5. 'The growth of the American West from 1850 was at an incredible pace throughout the territories.' Use Source 2 and any other knowledge of the topic to discuss this.

6. What problems could this rapid growth create? Use your own knowledge from studying this book to help you.

GOVERNMENT

On 4 July 1776 the American Congress declared itself free of British control following the American War of Independence. You can see the original 13 states on the map on page 61. The new government set itself the task of establishing the means by which these states were to be governed. There was to be provision for the control of other territories further west and their potential incorporation within the Union at later dates. Here is an extract from the law for the organisation of new land in the West in 1787.

SOURCE 1

Be it ordained by the United States in Congress assembled, that the said territory . . . be one district . . . That there shall be appointed, from time to time by Congress, a governor . . . There shall also be appointed a court, to consist of three judges . . . The governor and judges shall adopt and publish in the district such laws of the original States . . . as may be necessary, and best suited to the circumstances of the district, and report them to Congress . . . As soon as the legal body shall be formed in the district, the council and house assembled shall have authority to elect a delegate to Congress . . . There shall be formed in the territory not less than three nor more than five States . . . And whenever any of the said States shall have sixty thousand free inhabitants, such States shall be admitted, by its delegation, into the United States.

The core of this was the Federal Government that dealt with important issues affecting all of the states, such as defence. The elected President wielded a great deal of power during his stay in office: there were 17 presidents during our period. Alongside the President was Congress that made the laws.

It was divided into two houses called the Senate and the House of Representatives that were made up of people elected from the states. Together, the President and Congress made all key decisions affecting the USA.

However, a great deal of power rested with Local State Governments, each based in the State's main city. A Governor controlled each state. The Governor and the State Government, both elected by the people, made most decisions affecting the state including law and order, and education. These powers gave states a great deal of freedom. The Territories that did not yet have sufficient people to apply to become a state, envied this: they were subject to far more direct control from the Federal Government. You can see this structure in Source 2.

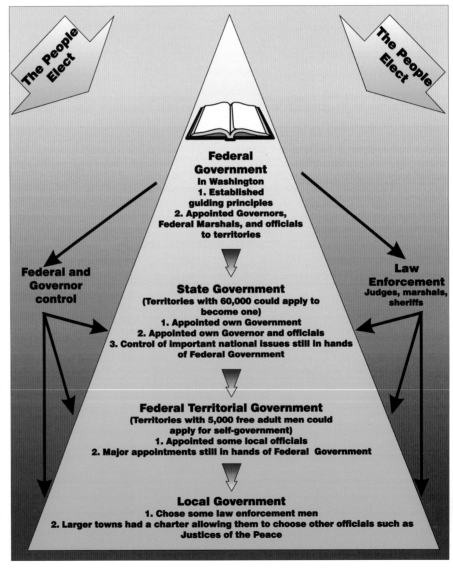

The People Elect

The People Elect

Federal Government
in Washington
1. Established guiding principles
2. Appointed Governors, Federal Marshals, and officials to territories

Federal and Governor control

Law Enforcement
Judges, marshals, sheriffs

State Government
(Territories with 60,000 could apply to become one)
1. Appointed own Government
2. Appointed own Governor and officials
3. Control of important national issues still in hands of Federal Government

Federal Territorial Government
(Territories with 5,000 free adult men could apply for self-government)
1. Appointed some local officials
2. Major appointments still in hands of Federal Government

Local Government
1. Chose some law enforcement men
2. Larger towns had a charter allowing them to choose other officials such as Justices of the Peace

SOURCE 2

Case Study 1 : A President
Abraham Lincoln (1809–65)

Lincoln was President from 1861 to 1865. He was President at a very difficult time. He co-ordinated the Union campaign against the South during the Civil War (1861–65) leading the North to victory. He fought hard to end slavery which was finally abolished in 1865. He also played a vital role in the Homestead Act of 1862 (see pages 22–23) which was to have a huge impact on settlement in the West. He displayed considerable skills in working with people in his government with very different beliefs and opinions. However, following an announcement that he favoured some blacks having the vote in one State, he was assassinated in 1865.

Case Study 2 : A Governor
Lew Wallace (1827–1905)

Wallace was Governor of New Mexico from 1878 to 1881. Like other Governors he came from a successful background. He fought in the Mexican War in 1848; and in the later Civil War he was a major general on the Union side. He then served in some military courts before being appointed Governor. He was faced with the aftermath of the Lincoln County War and issued an amnesty to those involved to end the unrest. He met with Billy the Kid to negotiate a deal which later fell through (see pages 71–73). During this time he was finishing his book *Ben Hur* which was to become immensely successful: it was made into a major film in 1959 and is still regularly shown on TV.

President Abraham Lincoln

Governor Lew Wallace

1. Use Source 2 and the text to write a paragraph on each of the following:

   Federal Government;

   State Government;

   Territorial/Local Government.

2. Why is Source 1 such an important historical source?

3. What does Source 3 tell us about the qualities needed to be a President or Governor?

4. 'Federal and State Government was the best system to control the USA.' Do you agree?

5. Does this module support the guiding principle 'Government by the people for the people'?

WAS THE WEST LAWLESS?

SOURCE 1

The engine had hardly stopped when I jumped on the running-board on one side . . . As soon as the engineer and fireman saw our guns they threw up their hands without being told . . . I shoved my gun against the official's nose and put him to work . . . There was only $900 in the safe. That was mightily small winnings for our trouble, so we decided to go through the passengers . . . Jim held the passengers steady while I searched the berths . . . There were many watches, bracelets, rings and pocket-books . . . We ordered everybody back to bed, told 'em good night very politely at the door, and left. We rode 40 miles before daylight and then divided up the stuff.

O. Henry, c.1890.

Sources 1 and 2 depict violent images of lawlessness. How typical were these sources of life in the American West? Let us develop this further by examining the question: Was the West lawless?

SOURCE 2

'Smoke of a .45', a painting by Charles M. Russell, 1908.

Was the West lawless?

Lawmen

Townspeople often thought it was better to appoint a 'badman' as lawman than risk an ineffective 'goodman'. Also, the job could be very profitable: corrupt Sheriff John Gehan apparently got $40,000 a year. These 'perks' of the job attracted the wrong type of people as this historian wrote in 1988:

'A sheriff who wore a tin badge one day might be swinging from a tree for cattle rustling the next, lynched by the very people whose lives he was protecting – and whose cattle he was stealing.'

Judges

Some frightened judges allowed criminals to escape justice. One judge in 1840 left a note saying he was too frightened to stay: he was found shot dead a few days later. Even courtrooms could be subject to fights and disorder. One judge ordered that 'any person caught throwing turnips, cigar stubs, beets, or old bits of tobacco at this court will be immediately arrested'.

Some local juries hated outside interference and refused to convict criminals tried by outsider judges. Many justices of the peace and judges could be bribed. When the law was carried out it could be violent and horrific, as the career of Judge Parker showed. Sixty five of his deputies were killed while he was in office. He had a special gallows built to hold 12 men: crowds of 5,000 turned up to watch hangings, appalling people in the East. Even the lawyers were far from perfect. Some were ignorant of the law – the best ones tended to work in the East that offered the best paid jobs.

Vigilantes often took the law into their own hands. In San Francisco a vigilante committee in 1851 arrested 89 people: four were hung and one whipped. The committee formed again in 1856 with over 6,000 volunteers. It formed its own political party, backed by businessmen, who saw to it that taxes for business were cut even when this meant closing schools. In 1884, during a ranch war, Montana ranchers lynched 35 for cattle rustling.

This statement was made by gunslinger Bill Longely in 1877 before his execution.

'There was no law at all . . . When the majority of people got down on a man, they simply took him out and strung him up on a limb, and they had a big spree on the strength of it.'

Lawmen

Law enforcement was established by the federal government, summed up by an expert in 1974:

'Collectively, the town, county, territorial or state, and federal lawmen made up a sizeable hierarchy, with the US marshal at the top of the pecking order.'

Many lawmen were of good character and did their jobs well, helped by townsfolk when necessary. Sheriffs carried out a range of tasks such as maintaining the county jail and selling the property of tax debtors. Marshals acted as fire inspectors, health inspectors, and collected licences for saloons in addition to the work of catching criminals. Source 3 shows the first lawmen in Guthrie, Oklahoma.

Judges

Criminals were dealt with severely if convicted: either a long prison sentence or execution. A good example is Judge Charles Parker who was appointed to Indian Territory and took his work very seriously. He tried to help the Indians who had few legal rights. He became known as the Hanging Judge, and in two decades he sentenced 160 people to death.

Vigilante groups were very common and, some believe, misunderstood. Most meant to do well at a time before legal federal law had arrived. One schoolmaster said:

'It is lawful for citizens to slay robbers and murders when they catch them; or ought they to wait for the policemen, when there are none, or put them in prisons not yet built?'

In mining communities there was a serious attempt to organise some form of legal system where none existed in the absence of proper government. Miners' courts were set up firstly to protect the claims of the miners, as this contemporary account shows.

'The laws laid down by a miners' court were very simple and absolutely just. There were no appeals from the court's decisions. These early day miners were men of unquestionable honesty and there was little willingness to go against the rights of others. Consequently the law was followed to the letter.'

Some miners' courts dealt with a range of crimes. Meetings were held to choose a judge and jury. However, these courts could not deal with serious crimes caused by hardened criminals flocking to mining settlements.

Criminals

Studying criminals can be chilling, as these comments by historians show.

'The loners frequently murdered out of sudden impulse. They appeared to lack any semblance of self-control . . . and inner check that told them when to stop . . . Nor did the loners suffer any evident remorse.'

'He is the terror of all who come near him, his visits to the frontier towns . . . being regarded as a calamity second only to a western tornado.'

Source 5 is a wanted poster. His own man shot Jesse James dead in 1882 for the reward.

Criminals

One expert estimated that there were perhaps no more than 20 lone killers on the frontier. Their crimes have given a false impression of what life was like, mainly as modern writers and the media have focused so much on their exploits, such as the criminal career of Billy the Kid (see pages 71–73). Source 4 shows a scene in a Tombstone saloon that contradicts the common modern idea that they were filled with violence.

SOURCE 3

Arizona Rangers, 1885.

SOURCE 4

Gambling in the saloon, Arizona, 1895.

SOURCE 5

REWARD

$15,000 REWARD
FRANK JAMES
DEAD or ALIVE

$25,000 REWARD FOR JESSE JAMES

$5000 Reward for any Known Member of the James Band

SIGNED

ST. LOUIS MIDLAND RAILROAD

'Wanted' poster for Frank and Jesse James.

1. What impression do Sources 1 and 2 give of the American West?

2. Make and complete the following table:

Good			Bad
	Lawmen		
	Judges/vigilantes		

3. In what ways do the pictorial sources give conflicting ideas about lawlessness in the West?

4. Was the West lawless? Use the evidence from this module and any other knowledge you have to discuss this in an essay.

Wyatt Earp: Lawman or criminal?

In the previous unit we considered how lawless the West really was. The next units look at case studies to help you refine your opinion.

Wyatt Earp (Source 6) became marshal of Dodge City (see page 37). He banned weapons in the town, and enforced this with brutality if necessary, with several arrests every day. Earp's very tough approach was successful in calming the town in only eight months, though some felt he went too far. However, his best known job was as Deputy US Marshal in Tombstone, Arizona, which led to the notorious Gunfight at the OK Corral.

SOURCE 7

On a blustery day towards the end of October 1881, the town of Tombstone, Arizona, witnessed the most notorious shoot-out in the history of the West. In a vacant lot at the rear of the OK Corral, City Marshal Virgil Earp and his brothers Wyatt and Morgan, joined by a gambler friend, Doc Holliday, exchanged gunfire with four local cowboys, the Clanton and McLaury brothers . . . The

SOURCE 6

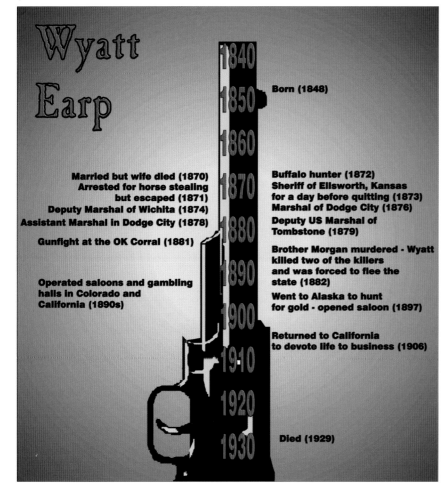

duration was slightly more than half a minute, although a deadly staccato of vengeful gunfire echoed for months afterwards.

Paul Trachtman, The Gunfighters, 1974.

The Earps 'won', but were arrested for murder: they were all acquitted. The blood lust continued when Morgan Earp was murdered. Wyatt sought revenge and murdered two of the gang forcing him to flee the state as an outlaw, still determined to kill the others although he never achieved this. Two conflicting sources show how divided people were at the time (Sources 8 and 9).

SOURCE 8

Wyatt Earp is equally famous in the cheerful business of depopulating the country. He has killed within our personal knowledge six men, and he is popularly accredited with relegating to the dust no less than ten of his fellow men.

Newspaper article, 1881.

SOURCE 9

During his whole stay here he occupied a place of high social position and was regarded as a high-minded, honourable citizen. As Marshal of our city he was ever vigilant in carrying out his duties: he was brave, unflinching, and on all occasions proved himself the right man in the right place.

Petition to the Judge signed by the people of Dodge City, 1881.

Since then Wyatt Earp has become one of the heroes of the West and has been featured in many films and books. Does he deserve to be called a hero?

---

1. Use the information in this unit to write a short biography of Wyatt Earp.

2. Was Wyatt Earp a lawman or a criminal?

WAR IN JOHNSON COUNTY!

WAR!

Stop Press : Trouble in Wyoming

Trouble has been brewing for years in Johnson County, Wyoming. Cattlemen want more power. They face problems caused by a government that does not understand that poor quality Wyoming land means far more is needed for each individual to make a living. A call to give cattlemen 2,560 acres of free semi-arid land was turned down by Congress who didn't understand that this was less than 160 acres of good land. Cattlemen have begun taking land for themselves. With homesteaders arriving since the early 1880s, rustlers taking their cattle, and the dreadful winter of 1886–87, cattlemen are desperate . . .

Stop Press : Sickening lynchings

A gang in 1889 lynched James Averell – a quiet and popular man – and Ella Watson – a prostitute. The lynchings have caused great disquiet. It is generally thought that the cattlemen are behind this outrage as Watson had a small number of cattle which she had re-branded. Averell was on land that the cattlemen want for themselves.

Stop Press : Is no-one safe?

When Wyoming joined the Union in 1890 fear struck at the heart of this community. A man was killed in June 1891, and later that year, in November, two men were attacked by cattlemen. That same month another two men were ambushed and murdered, apparently for cattle rustling. Attempts to bring the accused to justice have failed. Many people believe that the accusations of cattle rustling were mostly made up as an excuse for cattlemen to grab more power. Homesteaders hate the cattlemen even more: the two sides are dangerously far apart.

Stop Press : Invaders

Between 1891 and 1892 a handful of

Artist's impression of the lynching of Averell and Watson.

cattlemen organised a search-and-destroy mission. The expedition included nine big cattlemen, 13 ranch foremen, five stock detectives, 22 mercenaries from Texas, two newspaper reporters, and four observers. They called themselves 'Regulators': others called them 'Invaders'. Their objective was simple: to destroy all opposition. They carried with them a list of all those who had to be killed, including lawmen.

We turn now to the most reliable account of what happened, taken from the *Buffalo Bulletin* of April 1892.

'On the night of April 6 there arrived . . . a special train loaded with men . . . Before daylight the party came in this direction. In the testimony given before the coroner's jury there were 52 men in the party . . . Before daylight on the morning of 9 April this party of cattle barons and their hired assassins arrived near Nolan's Ranch on Powder River, known as the KC Ranch . . . There were in said ranch Nathan D. Champion, Nicholas Ray, Ben Johnson a trapper and others.

'Shortly before daylight, Johnson stepped out of the door and was captured . . . Champion then fought off the crowd until nearly 4 p.m. . . . The cattle barons . . . took a wagon, loaded it

Photograph of the 'Regulators', 1892

with pitch pine, set it afire and ran it against the house . . . setting the building on fire, and Champion when he could no longer endure the smoke, ran from the building, and was soon riddled with bullets.

'Sunday . . . it was reported in Buffalo that the invaders were at the TA Ranch'. . . That evening 49 men rode out of town . . . and arrived at the TA about midnight. Pickets were posted around the building . . . and the party waited for daylight. The whole posse took positions in sheltered places on all sides of the ranch . . . shots were fired by the besieged cattlemen and the battle was on.

'Sheriff Angus returned to Buffalo early Monday morning.' At the head of about 40 more men he proceeded to the TA and assumed command of the posse. Reinforcements continued to come in hourly . . . until about 250 men were assembled under the sheriff.

'Tuesday . . . Colonel Van Horn . . . then advanced on the fortifications waving a flag of truce. Major Walcott, commanding the cattle barons' party, came from the fortifications, refused to surrender to Sheriff Angus, but surrendered to Col Van Horn . . . The invaders were disarmed, and . . . were . . . held under guard.'

Stop Press : Where is justice?

It is painful to report that none of those arrested was convicted. There have been rumours that the judge was under the control of cattle barons. By January 1893 the case was dismissed and the Invaders released. Feelings run high in Buffalo but it seems that justice is not to be done. At least it is unlikely that the cattle barons will try anything like this again.

1. a) Where did this 'WAR!' happen?
   b) What did each side accuse the other of doing/wanting?
2. Describe what trouble happened between 1889 and 1891.
3. Describe who the Regulators/Invaders were and what happened.

4. Historians' views have differed. One wrote: 'the comic Johnson County War ended before it got started'. Another said: 'It was this, more than anything else, that ended the rule of the cattle barons'. How important was the War? What can we learn from it? Use this unit and other knowledge you have to answer this as a short essay.

KEY BIOGRAPHIES

Frémont: hero or glory-seeker?

John Frémont (1813–90) was a trailblazer who mapped the way for thousands of people going west. Some journeys were made in the winter over mountains in appalling conditions, risking lives to map hostile areas. His surveys and adventures became famous as he pushed himself on to greater things, including the military and politics (Source 1). However, some people believe that the adventures disguise failures, recklessness, and a desire to show-off regardless of the cost. Source 2 summarises his career by looking at both sides of the argument. Use these to judge for yourself whether Frémont was a hero or a reckless glory-seeker.

SOURCE 1

He became a living symbol for the Manifest Destiny movement . . . He was such a glamorous, persuasive, appealing figure that he aroused the westering impulse of the American people as no other man ever did before or after him . . . John Charles Frémont was a man of immense influence in the development of the West.

Bill Gilbert, The Trailblazers, *1973.*

SOURCE 2

Good	Bad
Joined Corps of Engineers in 1838.	Lost vital records in 1842 shooting rapids on River Platte which he did not even need to be on.
Married senator's daughter in 1841.	Took a huge howitzer gun 4,800km on expedition, probably to look impressive.
He made five dangerous expeditions into the West between 1842–54.	Ignored orders in winter of 1844 to go to Oregon. Went to California in dreadful weather. Had to eat horses.
Climbed the second highest peak, the Wind River Mountains, in 1842.	Wrongly described Utah as very fertile. Mormons settled there on his recommendation.
1843 Report well received by Congress.	Fled from Mexicans in 1854. One man said he was 'the most complete coward I ever knew'.
Formed the Californian Battalion during war with Mexico.Seized land for the USA.	Refused orders from Washington to disband his Californian Battalion and was court-martialled.
Purchased Californian land later found to have gold.	He ignored all advice to turn back in 1848 winter survey. Ten men died.
Became very wealthy.	Voted out of the Senate in 1850 after serving 21 working days.
Represented California in the Senate in 1850.	Failed presidential candidate in 1856 and 1864.
Supported anti-slavery movement.	Proved a bungling general during the Civil War and lost his command.
Presidental candidate in 1856 and 1864.	Ran his Californian estates badly and went bankrupt.
Governor of Arizona 1879–83.	
Restored to rank of major-general in 1890.	

1. Describe Frémont's work under these headings:
    trailblazer;
    soldier;
    politician.

2. a) Study Source 2. Why is it possible to produce such different accounts of Frémont?

    b) What problems does this type of conflicting information pose historians?

3. 'Hero or Glory-seeker?' Use the evidence to write a balanced account of Frémont and his career.

BILLY THE KID

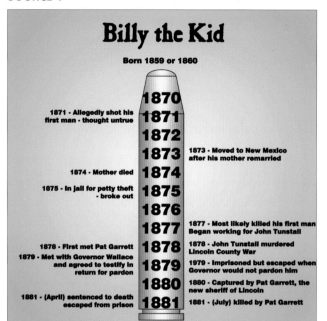

Billy the Kid

Born 1859 or 1860

1871 - Allegedly shot his first man - thought untrue	**1870** **1871**
	1872
	1873 1873 - Moved to New Mexico after his mother remarried
1874 - Mother died	**1874**
1875 - In jail for petty theft - broke out	**1875**
	1876
1877 - Most likely killed his first man Began working for John Tunstall	**1877**
1878 - First met Pat Garrett	**1878** 1878 - John Tunstall murdered Lincoln County War
1879 - Met with Governor Wallace and agreed to testify in return for pardon	**1879** 1979 - Imprisoned but escaped when Governor would not pardon him
	1880 1880 - Captured by Pat Garrett, the new sheriff of Lincoln
1881 - (April) sentenced to death escaped from prison	**1881** 1881 - (July) killed by Pat Garrett

SOURCE 2

Photograph of Billy.

There are a few people who capture the public imagination so much that it is difficult to separate the person from the legend. In the history of the American West Billy the Kid falls into this category. We shall examine the facts, the myth, and try to see if Billy matched the myth.

We know very little about his early life (Sources 1 and 2): we do not even know what his real name was for certain. His first imprisonment came in 1875 shortly after the death of his mother left him an orphan. This was to have a great effect on him. His imprisonment only lasted a few days before he broke out of jail: a trend he was to repeat. In 1877 a blacksmith teased Billy one time too many and Billy shot him. Billy was imprisoned, and Billy escaped again.

He went to work for an Englishman, John Tunstall, as a cattle guard. Tunstall was good to Billy who perhaps

SOURCE 3

The original cover of Pat Garrett's book, An Authentic Life of Billy the Kid, *1882.*

saw Tunstall as a parent figure. Billy was then caught up in the so-called Lincoln County War over the lucrative beef trade. Tunstall was on the side of Alexander McSween, who had the support of the powerful rancher John Chisum. Their opponents were a pair of corrupt politicians and cattle barons who controlled Sheriff Brady. Brady had Tunstall murdered. This event was a watershed in Billy's life as he began a vicious vendetta. He murdered Brady. He also murdered others who were involved in Tunstall's murder even though they had surrendered. This blood lust continued until Billy, McSween and others were besieged in a house for several days before McSween was killed. This ended the Lincoln County War and Billy's mission.

The new Governor – Lew Wallace (see page 63) – offered pardons to those involved in the recent 'War'. However, Billy had other crimes to answer for. He met with the Governor and struck a deal: he would testify against other men in return for a pardon. Wallace agreed. Billy allowed himself to be captured, but soon discovered that he would not be pardoned. He escaped from jail again.

The final part of the story started in 1880 when an old drinking friend – Pat Garrett – was appointed Sheriff of Lincoln County and ordered to track Billy down. Billy was caught and sentenced to death in April 1881 before escaping again, killing two law officers in the process. He was pursued by Garrett, whom some historians think was incapable of doing very much. A tip-off led to Billy being found at Fort Sumner where Garrett shot him dead. Billy claimed that he had killed 21 men.

Our problem begins with the first book written about Billy by Pat Garrett in 1882 (Source 3). Historians agree that Garrett did not write the book alone. It was written with a drunken printer – Ash Upson – who appears to have written the first part himself, and which is generally considered to be mainly fiction.

SOURCE 4

This book, far more than all the dime novels written about the Kid, is responsible for continuing unproved tales about his early life . . . If Ash knew the facts, they evidently were laid aside in favour of trying to outdo the writers of 'yellow-covered cheap novels'.

J. C. Dykes (ed.), Pat Garrett: The Authentic Life of Billy the Kid, *1954.*

This book was followed by many cheap sensational books which were based on Garrett's book and on fantasy to sell copies (Source 5). One million were sold within a year of Billy's death.

SOURCE 5

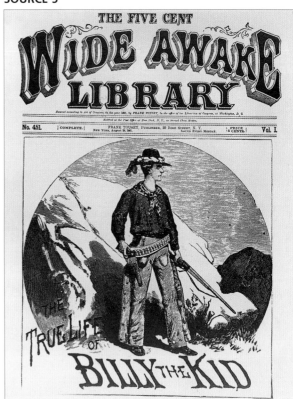

Cover of a 'dime novel' about Billy the Kid published in 1881.

SOURCE 6

Hundred of articles, radio and TV shows, stories, books and motion pictures have been written around this unique young man. Unfortunately none of the writers had access to more than a small part of the hidden source material which would have cleared away the fabulous tales and obscure half-truths and brought into clear focus the real Billy the Kid and the great days he lived.

Frazier Hunt, The Tragic Days of Billy the Kid, *1956.*

Source 7 comes from *Pat Garrett and Billy the Kid* (1973), a film that depicted Billy as a killer, but also as a likeable and very popular person. Notice that the actor playing Billy (on the left) was in his late 30s – almost twice Billy's actual age! Today Billy even has his own Internet site.

Now look at what some people have written about Billy to see if he deserves his reputation.

SOURCE 8

There were no bounds to his generosity. Friends, strangers, and even his enemies, were welcome to his money, his horse, his clothes, or anything else of which he happened, at the time, to possess.

Pat Garrett, The Authentic Life of Billy the Kid, *1882.*

SOURCE 7

PAT GARRETT AND BILLY THE KID x Starring JAMES COBURN - KRISS KRISTOFFERSON - DYLAN   METROCOLOR ®   PANAVISION ®   Released by M

This advertising material is licensed and not sold and is the Property of National Screen Service Ltd. and upon completion of the exhibition for which it has been licensed it should be returned to National

Still from the film Pat Garrett and Billy the Kid, *1973.*

SOURCE 11

The attention riveted on Billy is hard to explain. His lifetime score of men killed was much lower (than others – probably 9). Even his fierceness was patently of an inferior order – at the start, anyway . . . For the fact was that, at the worst of his deadly career, he was a downy-cheeked, blue-eyed orphan lad whose engaging and innocent grin won over the motherly concern of women and made men want to help him however they could. But a killer he was, and that smiling young countenance made this truth all the more grotesque.

Paul Trachtman, The Gunfighters, *1974.*

SOURCE 9

Billy the Kid took sides with the people of the country, to fight for our property and our lives. He stood with us to the end, brave and reliable . . . He had a wonderful presence of mind; the tighter the place the more he showed his cool nerve and quick brain . . . At the beginning he was not the blood-thirsty, hard desperado that history has made him out to be. That he ever killed as many men as he is given credit for, or ever killed for money, is absurd. He never seemed to care for money, except to buy cartridges with . . . He never drank . . . and he never used tobacco in any form.

Frank Coe (who rode with Billy).

SOURCE 10

The Kid certainly didn't look the part of a killer . . . He weighed only a trifle more than 130 pounds (59kg) . . . He was good-natured and of a happy carefree disposition, and there are proofs galore of his genuine kindness of heart to old people, children, and poor Mexicans.

Frazier Hunt, The Tragic Days of Billy the Kid, *1956.*

1. Use the text and timeline to write an account of Billy the Kid's life under these headings:

   1859–1876; 1877–1880; 1881.

2. What problems do historians have in finding out about Billy?

3. How reliable are Sources 3, 5 and 7 in finding out about him?

4. a) Copy out and fill in using Sources 8 to 11.

Source	Good points	Bad points

   b) Do these provide enough evidence to decide what Billy was really like?

5. 'Billy the Kid was just a ruthless killer who had a cute smile and polite manners.' Do you agree?

CHARLES GOODNIGHT: 'FATHER OF THE COWBOYS'

This is the story of a young boy brought to Texas at around 10 years old in 1846 having ridden bareback for 1,000 km because his family were too poor to afford a saddle. He was to become one of the wealthiest and most important cattlemen in the American West. He was Charles Goodnight (Source 1). Goodnight soon got into the cattle business but it was hardly profitable (Source 2).

SOURCE 1

Charles Goodnight.

SOURCE 2

'As the end of the first year's branding resulted in only 32 calves for our share, and as the value was about $3 per head, we figured out that we had made between us, not counting expenses, $96.'

He joined the Texas Rangers and fought for the Confederacy during the Civil War. The South was exhausted by 1865. All that Goodnight had of value were his longhorn cattle. As we have seen, the numbers of cattle soared during the Civil War. Goodnight's had grown to 8,000 though he knew he would only get a few rounded up.

SOURCE 3

'I suffered great losses. The Confederate authorities had taken many of them without paying a cent. Indians had raided our herds and cattle thieves were branding them, to their own benefit without regard to our rights.'

Texas prices were low, at $8–$10 a head; in some mining regions, however, people would pay $60. Goodnight decided to take his cattle to this new market. He was joined by veteran Oliver Loving. Loving had prospered during the Civil War by selling beef to Confederate forces. He now joined Goodnight in 1866 to trail cattle to New Mexico: the beginning of the Long Drives. The path they used soon became known as the Goodnight–Loving Trail (see map on page 31). Their first expedition netted them more than $12,000! However, this and later trails were fraught with dangers, especially from Indian raids and stampedes. During the second trail in 1867 Loving was shot through the wrist by an Indian and later died of gangrene. Goodnight gives an idea of the dangers describing a stampede when the mule carrying all their gold and supplies bolted:

SOURCE 4

'I grabbed a rope that was dangling from the pack and checked the frantic animal after being dragged quite a distance down a rocky slope at the risk of a broken neck. The gold was saved, but our provisions were entirely lost, and there was no way to get them renewed.'

By 1870 Goodnight decided to make a change from trailing: 'After I married I thought I would no longer follow my wild trail life. I concluded to settle down and take up ranching instead.' Around this time he also bought extensive land near Pueblo, Colorado. By this time he was making sufficient money to go into banking, although this turned sour when many banks failed in the Panic of 1873, leaving him almost penniless. However, his determination was such that he was willing to gamble by taking out a huge loan of $30,000. The man who loaned him this money – John Adair – became his business partner; and together they began the famous JA Ranch, keeping up their partnership for 11 years. Goodnight began crossing longhorns with Hereford cattle that produced more meat, milk and profit. Men were needed to look after the 100,000 cattle. He wrote: 'To care for them over such an extensive range we employed a little army of men called "cowboys".' Goodnight was one of the first to use this term: before this they had simply been called 'boys'.

In order to be successful, Goodnight had to be ruthless. In 1876 he took over a huge expanse of land and simply told his neighbours what was his and what was theirs as the nearest law was 200 miles away. The next year he bought 12,000 acres of public land. In order to keep others out he bought all the areas with water, hay and good building sites, making the rest useless for anyone else to buy – so he could graze his animals there. By 1888 he was worth over $500,000.

As he got older he tended to treat his cowboys like children, forbidding them to drink alcohol, gamble, or even use bad language: however, the effect of this was that his cowboys tended to go wild when they hit Dodge City after a long drive. Goodnight died in 1929.

John Iliff

One of Goodnight's main customers was John Iliff, who bought 30,000 cattle from him over ten years. In 1859 Iliff had gone to the gold mines in Colorado selling stores and grazing cattle. He sold beef extensively to railroad camps, making him enough capital to go into large-scale ranching. He also made use of the new railroads to ship beef packed in ice to cities in the East. He became one of the largest operators, with 25,000 grazing cattle and employing 40 to 50 cowboys. By importing Durham and Hereford bulls from England he was able to produce high-quality beef, often selling at $50 a head.

1. What do Sources 2 and 3 tell us about Charles Goodnight's early problems?

2. a) Why did he begin to drive cattle?

   b) How successful was the first drive?

   c) What was the Goodnight–Loving Trail?

   d) What dangers did they face?

3. Describe the main points of his partnership with John Adair.

4. How could he be ruthless?

5. Write short biographies on John Iliff and Oliver Loving using this unit and any other information you have.

6. a) This unit includes extracts from Goodnight's own words. How useful are autobiographical sources to historians?

   b) What limitations are there in using autobiographies?

7. 'Charles Goodnight was a hero of the West.' Do you agree?

'MYTHICAL' WOMEN

Calamity Jane

Martha Jane Cannary (Source 1) was born in 1852. Her mother died around 1866, followed shortly afterwards by her father. Her reputation developed as she refused to follow the stereotypical image of a woman. She frequently dressed in men's clothes, drank heavily, chewed tobacco, swore, and used a gun. She acquired her nickname 'Calamity Jane' around this time: some said that this was because calamity would follow any man who upset her. However, despite acting tough she could be very kind: during an epidemic of smallpox in 1878 she nursed the sick day and night, making her very popular among those who knew her. She went on a geological expedition into the Black Hills in 1875 but was sent home for swimming naked with the men. From 1896 she appeared in Wild Bill's Wild West Shows. However, the other side of Calamity Jane was that she was a 'camp follower' (prostitute). More serious was her severe drinking problem; this helped to ensure that by 1901 she was ill and poverty-stricken. Calamity Jane died two years later.

In order to cash in on her fame, Calamity wrote an autobiography that she sold on her travels. Here are some extracts to give you an idea what she said about herself.

SOURCE 1

A photo of Martha Jane Cannary (Calamity Jane) in men's clothing.

SOURCE 2

Joined General Custer as a scout at Fort Russell, Wyoming, in 1870, and started for Arizona for the Indian campaign . . .

Was in Arizona up to the winter of 1871 and during that time I had a great many adventures with the Indians . . .

During the month of June (1876) I acted as a pony express rider carrying the US mail between Deadwood and Custer . . .

In 1879 I went to Fort Pierre and drove trains (of oxen) from Rapid City to Fort Pierre for Frank Witcher . . .

In 1881 I went to Wyoming and returned in 1882 to Miles City and took up a ranch on the Yellowstone, raising stock and cattle.

Accounts of her adventures brought her to the attention of 'dime novel' publishers, and exciting tales soon appeared in print. However, her autobiography was very dangerous to accept unless it was supported by other sources: regretfully, some writers chose to accept it at face value and did not check its reliability. Had they done so they would have come to a very different impression of Calamity Jane, as the historian in Source 3 explains.

SOURCE 3

Virtually everything in it . . . has been disputed. Some of the incidents are proved impossible by eyewitnesses and contemporary accounts. Nearly all of her story of scouting and dispatch riding is merely ludicrous.

Robert J. Casey, The Black Hills and Their Incredible Characters, *1949.*

The myth that has grown up around her is false. Commenting on her death another historian wrote: 'So passed the woman who probably gained more notoriety, with less good reason, than any other female character in all of the old West.'

Annie Oakley

Our second woman also toured with Wild West shows; she also used a gun. Beyond this she was nothing like Calamity Jane. Annie Oakley was born in 1860 in Ohio into a very poor family of Quakers with her father dying when she was four. Two years later she began to teach herself to shoot to provide food for her family and to sell her kills. Her shooting skills became so good that by 1875 she could beat all of the men. In that year she met Frank Butler who was a travelling marksman. He was not only very impressed by her skills, he fell in love with Annie and married her the next year: their marriage lasted nearly 50 years. Butler also became her manager to help her develop her potential as Annie rapidly became famous as a professional game hunter.

Between 1885 and 1902 Annie worked with Buffalo Bill's Wild West Show (Source 4), making many friends, including Sitting Bull who called her 'Little Sure Shot'. Indeed, she was so good that at 30 paces she could slice the thin edge of a playing card. She could even roll a tin can along the ground with shots from her two revolvers. Annie travelled abroad with the show in 1889 captivating the imagination of many, including Queen Victoria. In Berlin she shot ashes off a cigarette held in the mouth of Kaiser (King) Wilhelm. However, disaster struck in 1901 when she was involved in a train crash that left her partially paralysed. It took two years for her to discover that she could still shoot well. She spent the rest of her career working in variety shows.

Throughout her life Annie kept a strict moral code. She would not even wear make-up during her shows – and she managed not to let showbusiness spoil her life. Assessments of her are kinder than those about Calamity Jane.

Annie Oakley died in 1926. Twenty years later the musical *Annie Get Your Gun* turned her into a mythical woman by rewriting her character and life in Hollywood style.

SOURCE 4

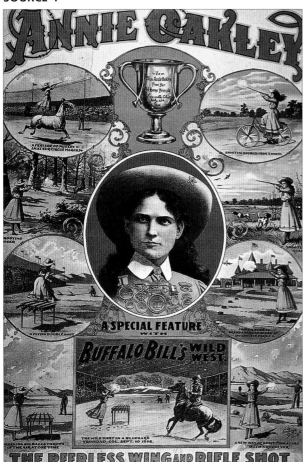

Poster for Buffalo Bill's Wild West show, advertising Annie Oakley.

SOURCE 5

A) Annie Oakley became an American legend in her own lifetime, but many misconceptions about her exist today. She was not the rip-roaring, man-chasing woman of loose morals portrayed in some movies and stage plays. She was a beautiful, talented, sensible woman whose shooting skills have rarely been equalled . . . She was a performer who remained happily married, sober and solvent.

Maturity USA Internet Site, 1996.

B) [She was a combination] of dainty feminine charm and lead bullets, draped in gorgeous yellow buckskin and topped with a halo of powder-blue smoke.

Stewart H. Holbrook, Little Annie Oakley and other Rugged People, *1948.*

---

1. Copy out and complete the following table.

Feature	Calamity Jane	Annie Oakley
Date of birth		
Date of death		
Family background		
Type of work		
Character		

---

2. Explain why Calamity Jane does not deserve her reputation.

3. Do you believe that Annie Oakley deserves her modern reputation (Source 5)?

4. Do you agree that these are both 'mythical women'?

BLOOD ON THE PLAINS

Why did war break out?

The hopes of peace, agreed at Fort Laramie in 1851 (page 39), were not to be. Within three years the Treaty was broken, and the second half of the century was stained in the blood of Indians and US soldiers (Sources 1 and 2). To understand these terrible events, we have to understand the nature of these wars (Source 3).

The historian who wrote Source 3 estimated that US troops were involved in 938 of these 'fights' between 1865 and 1898, meaning that a soldier was engaged in a serious conflict once every five years! We will only be looking at a few of these. Let's begin by tracing the main causes of the wars using accounts produced at the time.

SOURCE 3

These encounters were not wars in any traditional sense. Mostly they were skirmishes, small pitched battles, quick-strike manoeuvres. Many were called massacres, but the word was too charged emotionally, and its application tended to depend on whose side was involved . . . The simplest way to describe the conflicts . . . is to call them 'fights'.

Gerald F. Kreyche, Visions of the American West, *1989.*

SOURCE 4

A) This war was brought upon us by the children of the Great Father [US President] who came to take our land from us without price, and who, in our land, do a great deal many evil things . . . It has been our wish to live in our country peaceably . . . but the Great Father has filled it with soldiers who think only of our death.

Spotted Tail, Sioux.

B) What treaty that the Whites have kept has the Red Man broken? Not one. What treaty that the White Man has made with us have they kept? Not one.

Sitting Bull.

C) Along this border has been an almost incessant struggle, the Indians to retain and the whites to get possession; the war being broken by periods of occasional and temporary peace, which usually followed treaties whereby Indians agreed to surrender large tracts of their lands. This peace would continue until the land surrendered had been occupied by the whites, when the pressure of emigration would again break over the border, and the Indians by force or treaty, be compelled to surrender another portion of their cherished hunting grounds.

Report of the Secretary of the Interior, 1876.

To make this confusing period easier to understand, it has been divided into four key phases.

SOURCE 1

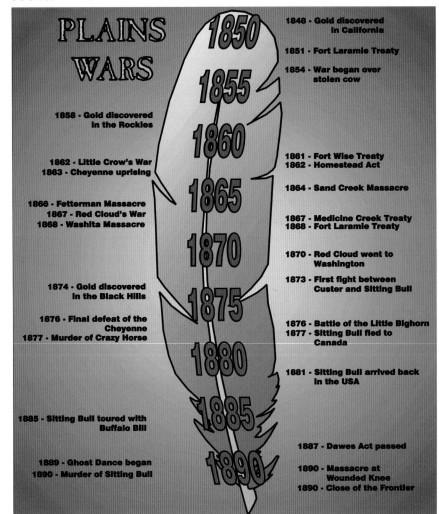

PLAINS WARS

- 1848 · Gold discovered in California
- 1850
- 1851 · Fort Laramie Treaty
- 1854 · War began over stolen cow
- 1855
- 1858 · Gold discovered in the Rockies
- 1860
- 1861 · Fort Wise Treaty
- 1862 · Homestead Act
- 1862 · Little Crow's War
- 1863 · Cheyenne uprising
- 1864 · Sand Creek Massacre
- 1865
- 1866 · Fetterman Massacre
- 1867 · Red Cloud's War
- 1868 · Washita Massacre
- 1867 · Medicine Creek Treaty
- 1868 · Fort Laramie Treaty
- 1870
- 1870 · Red Cloud went to Washington
- 1873 · First fight between Custer and Sitting Bull
- 1874 · Gold discovered in the Black Hills
- 1875
- 1876 · Final defeat of the Cheyenne
- 1877 · Murder of Crazy Horse
- 1876 · Battle of the Little Bighorn
- 1877 · Sitting Bull fled to Canada
- 1880
- 1881 · Sitting Bull arrived back in the USA
- 1885 · Sitting Bull toured with Buffalo Bill
- 1885
- 1887 · Dawes Act passed
- 1889 · Ghost Dance began
- 1890 · Murder of Sitting Bull
- 1890
- 1890 · Massacre at Wounded Knee
- 1890 · Close of the Frontier

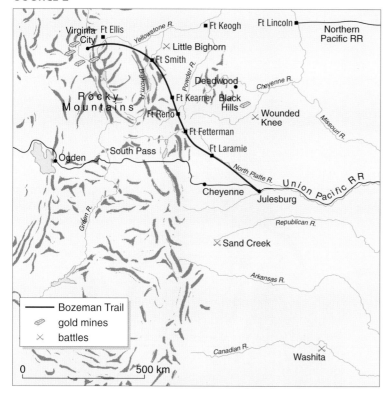

The Bozeman Trail and the lands of the Sioux.

Phase 1 : 1854–62

In 1854 Indians stole a cow from a Mormon and killed it. John L. Grattan, who was sent to sort it out, should have settled this minor incident. However, because of his poor judgement and a drunken anti-Indian interpreter, this incident sparked off a war, with 30 soldiers killed over the cow! It shows that both sides were far too eager to resort to violence. The fighting also showed a fatal flaw in the Indians' war strategy (Source 5).

SOURCE 5

The first battle between the Sioux and the whites revealed the fatal weakness of the Indians . . . Even the hot-blooded braves . . . would never have submitted to the discipline that alone could have made the follow-up campaign work.

Stephen E. Amboise, Crazy Horse and Custer, *1975.*

The main feature of this phase was Little Crow's War. Little Crow had taken on white ways: he even wore white clothing. However, as his people starved on their allocated land, his attitude hardened. A group of hungry Indian youths wanted to steal some settler's eggs. One of them was teased about his courage to do this, leading to the group killing the settler's family.

This forced Little Crow's hand and war followed. In a letter Little Crow accurately outlined his grievance:

SOURCE 6

We made a treaty with the government, and beg for what we get, and can't get that till our children are dying with hunger. It is the traders who commenced it. Mr A. J. Myrick told the Indians that they could eat grass or dung.

Little Crow, 1862. Myrick was later murdered with his mouth stuffed with grass.

The superiority of the US troops led to an Indian defeat and a sad recognition of this by Little Crow (Source 7). The situation had grown more desperate, and now the Californian Gold Rush was underway with thousands heading west. The Indians felt their existence was now under threat.

SOURCE 7

'I am ashamed to call myself a Sioux . . . Now we had better all run away and scatter out over the plains like buffalo and wolves. To be sure, the whites had wagon-guns and better arms than we, and there were many more of them. But that is no reason why we should not have beaten them, for we are brave Sioux and the whites are cowardly women.'

Phase 2 : 1863–68

The story now focuses on the Cheyenne who had established a peaceful reservation at Sand Creek, set up under the Fort Wise Treaty in 1861. Their leader, Black Kettle, had travelled to Washington and had been given a US flag from President Lincoln. However, the Sand Creek reservation was barren and soon his people were starving. This led to the Cheyenne murdering whites. This, in turn, led to about 300 Indians being butchered at Sand Creek by US troops in 1864 (see pages 86–87). This massacre triggered off more warfare that lasted until the Medicine Creek Treaty of 1867 by which several tribes agreed to give up lands and move onto reservations (see pages 90–91).

Then in December 1866 the foolish Captain William Fetterman led his troops into a Sioux trap in which he and a hundred of his men were killed, and mutilated so badly that the details were suppressed for 20 years. Source 8 shows how positions were hardening.

SOURCE 8

We must act with vindictive earnestness against the Sioux, even to their extermination – men, women, and children.

General Sherman, 1866.

The attack on Fetterman was master-minded by Red Cloud (Source 9) who now waged the most successful Indian war against the United States, spurred on by the surge of emigrants crossing Sioux lands, and a line of forts built to protect them. Two other highly skilled warriors joined him: Sitting Bull and Crazy Horse. The Government was forced to offer a new treaty (Source 10).

SOURCE 10

In the Spring of 1868 the Great Warrior Sherman and the peace commission returned to Fort Laramie. This time they had firm orders from an impatient government to abandon the forts on the Powder River and obtain a peace treaty with Red Cloud . . . Fort Phil Kearny was abandoned and the honour of burning it was given to the Cheyennes . . . After two years of resistance, Red Cloud had won his war . . . Now a conquering hero, he would sign the treaty
. . . [However] what many of the chiefs understood was in the treaty and what was actually written therein . . . were like two horses whose coloration did not match.

Dee Brown, Bury My Heart at Wounded Knee, *1970.*

Red Cloud. Photograph taken in 1880.

A major reason for proposing this treaty was Government concern that the Bozeman Trail should be free from attack as it linked the new gold fields. Red Cloud was the only Indian to get anything out of the 1867 and 1868 treaties. Even this success was soon to be eclipsed. Black Kettle had survived the Cheyenne Sand Creek Massacre and was now based in another peaceful camp on the Washita River. History was about to repeat itself.

SOURCE 11

A) Proceed to the Washita River . . . to destroy their villages and ponies; to kill all warriors, and to bring back all women and children.

Instructions to George Custer, 1868.

B) In a matter of minutes Custer's troops destroyed Black Kettle's village . . . To kill or hang all the warriors meant separating them from the old men, women, and children.

This work was slow and dangerous for the cavalrymen; they found it much more efficient and safe to kill indiscriminately. They killed 103 Cheyenne, but only eleven of them were warriors.

Dee Brown, Bury My Heart at Wounded Knee, *1970.*

SOURCE 12

The new decade began in 1870 with Red Cloud going to Washington where he met President Grant. It was here that he discovered that he had been tricked in 1868 when he heard the full terms of the Fort Laramie Treaty that bore no relation to what he had agreed. Nevertheless, this noble warrior honoured his pledge and retired to a reservation.

However, the most dramatic and destructive part of the struggle was still to take place.

SOURCE 13

An artist's impression of the Washita massacre in which Black Kettle was killed and scalped. Painted by Charles Schreyvogel in 1868.

1. What does Source 3 tell us about the wars?

2. Read Source 4. According to these writers, what caused the wars?

3. Phase 1: 1854–62

   a) What triggered the wars in 1854?

   b) What was wrong with Indian methods?

   c) What caused Little Crow's War?

   d) What was Little Crow's reaction to his defeat?

4. Phase 2: 1863–68

   a) What happened in: 1861; 1864; 1866; 1867?

   b) How does Source 10 show that the 1868 Fort Laramie Treaty was unfair?

   c) Use Sources 11 and 12 to explain what happened at Washita in 1868?

5. In what ways did life change for the Indians during this period?

   What aspects of their lives stayed the same?

6. Explain how each of the following played a part in the wars: ill-discipline; deception; revenge; mistrust; emotion.

7. 'It was clear by 1868 that the Indians were doomed to failure.' Do you agree?

THE WARMONGERS

In the biography section we looked at some of the people who gave life to the American West. No biography would be complete without some of the men who forged the West in blood: the men responsible for deciding upon war, and for carrying it out.

Sitting Bull (1831–90)

He was given his father's name – Sitting Bull – at 14 after he counted coup (see page 12). He became leader of the Teton Sioux in 1867, opposed to treaties with the whites giving away Sioux lands. He also strongly resisted attempts to force his people onto reservations. However, he was a good and kind man. One white friend said: 'As a friend he was sincere and true, as a patriot, devoted and incorruptible.'

After the Battle of the Little Bighorn he fled with his people to Canada in 1877 where the Canadians left them starving. He returned to the USA in 1881 after receiving false promises and was hastily imprisoned until 1885 when he was transferred to the Standing Rock reservation. In 1885 he joined Buffalo Bill Cody's Wild West show and toured in the USA and abroad. A year of this was enough and he returned to his people.

Later, Sitting Bull was wrongly seen as a major player in the Ghost Dance movement by the Government. While trying to arrest him in 1890, he and 12 of his men were killed. A missionary wrote: 'The . . . purpose of his life was to unify the tribes . . . and hold the remaining lands of his people as a sacred inheritance for their children. This fact made him unpopular with all who saw his policy and influence as an obstruction to their selfish schemes, hence they demanded his removal.'

Red Cloud (1822–1909)

He began as a warmonger and became a peacemaker. He spent his early years at war with other tribes, especially the Pawnee and Crow. We have already seen how successful he was in Red Cloud's War.

He did not join the other Sioux in their wars of 1876–77. Instead he tried to improve conditions on reservations; even managing to get a bad Indian Agent sacked. He did not encourage the Ghost Dance (see page 92), as he feared the consequences: as a result his people escaped the Army's purges. He fought for his people's rights until his death.

William Sherman (1820–91)

Sherman was a Civil War hero. He believed that Indians should be in reservations or killed. He once said: 'They all have to be killed or be maintained as a species of pauper.' He took this hostile attitude into the peace treaties in which he was involved.

In 1869 he became commander of the US Army. He pursued the policy of destroying the buffalo and attacking Indians during the winter when they were vulnerable. His Indian campaigns were successful in crushing Indian resistance on the Plains. He retired from the army in 1884.

Crazy Horse (1849–77)

He became famous for his ferocity in battle. Examples of the slaughter of his people made him even more determined to fight whites. He joined with Red Cloud and took part in the Fetterman Massacre. However, he was poor at maintaining military discipline.

He led his people to victory at the Battle of the Little Bighorn in 1876: unlike the other Sioux leaders he chose not to flee afterwards. A hard winter left his people desperate and led to his surrender in 1877. When he resisted imprisonment a US soldier murdered him.

George Custer (1839–76)

This flamboyant man graduated last from his military school class. However, he achieved notable successes during the Civil War. Afterwards, he was appointed lieutenant colonel of the Seventh Cavalry but was court-martialled for poor leadership. He redeemed himself in the Army's eyes in the Washita Massacre in 1868, and became famous for his undoubted personal bravery.

He was court-martialled again for desertion for leaving his company to visit his wife and was suspended for 10 months. He also fell out with President Grant and had to rely on friends to save his career.

He was sent to the Northern Plains to deal with the Lakota Sioux and protect railroad workers. In 1874 he was involved in protecting gold prospectors in the Indians' sacred Black Hills. His main claim to fame was at the Battle of the Little Bighorn when he and all of his men were killed.

Custer was lucky in having a wife who tirelessly promoted a glossy image of him until her death in 1933. Even today many see him as a hero. However increasing numbers question his ability: 'He undoubtedly possessed an enormous ego, ruthless ambition, and an unhealthy desire for self-glorification. There is also little doubt that at times . . . these personality traits affected his military judgement.' (*General Custer*, Castle Video *1994*)

Philip Sheridan (1831–88)

His success in the Civil War was followed by ruthless campaigns against the Indians. He shared Sherman's methods about subduing Indians, and was quite prepared to kill women and children if that made Indian defeats easier. He was behind the 1868 Washita Massacre.

He mounted highly successful attacks against Indians between 1874 and 1877, and became Commanding General of the US Army in 1884. He was credited for saying 'the only good Indians I ever saw were dead', although he denied it.

---

1. Write accounts under these headings based on this unit and your other knowledge of the topic:

a) US Army leaders;

b) Indian leaders.

---

2. a) What have the US Army leaders in common?

b) What have the Indian leaders in common?

3. What differences are there between the US Army leaders and the Indian leaders?

4. 'Both sides were made up of valiant leaders.' Do you agree?

THE BATTLE OF THE LITTLE BIGHORN

SOURCE 1

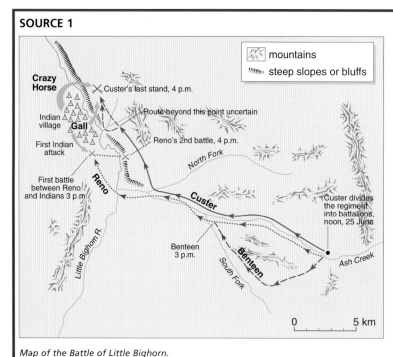

Map of the Battle of Little Bighorn.

Officer-in-charge: General Alfred Terry

Indians: Lakota Sioux and Cheyenne. Huge camp – around 12,000. Crazy Horse and Sitting Bull joined together.

Plan: Colonel John Gibbon's infantry to attack from the north. Custer's faster 7th Cavalry to attack from the south.

Outline of events on 25 June

- Scouts locate huge Indian village at dawn.
- Custer decides on immedite assault on village without waiting for Gibbon.
- Custer splits his men into three divisions, led by himself, Major Reno and Captain Benteen.
- Reno begins the assault unaware that Custer has changed his battle plans and would not support him. Forced back by the Sioux. Help comes from Benteen.
- Custer's five companies were isolated and annihilated.

Phase 3: 1869–76

Conflict exploded in 1874 when gold was discovered in the Black Hills of Dakota, sacred Indian land, protected by the Fort Laramie Treaty of 1868. Custer had been sent in to protect railroad surveyors when the gold was found. At first the US Government tried to keep prospectors out, but there were too many of them. The Government tried to do a deal with the Indians in 1875 offering $6 million, but this failed. The Government thought that the Indians were being unreasonable and hardened their attitude, demanding that all Indians go to their reservations: any who did not respond by 31 January 1876 would be treated as hostile. Many either did not hear about this threat or chose to ignore it, setting the scene for war.

In the summer of 1876 the US Army launched a campaign against the Indians which was to lead to the most stunning Indian victory: Custer's Last Stand at the Battle of the Little Bighorn. On 25 June all 225 of Custer's men were killed. When they were discovered two days later, their bodies were stripped and mutilated: only Custer was spared this out of respect of his bravery.

SOURCE 2

For Custer

'Custer acted under a misapprehension. He thought that the Indians were running. For fear that they might get away he attacked without getting all his men up, and divided his men so they were beaten.'
General Alfred H. Terry.

The conduct of the officers throughout was excellent . . . It is the conclusion of this court, in view of all the facts, that no further proceedings are necessary.
Findings of Court of Inquiry.

'It was common belief that the Sioux would, upon the appearance of the troops, hasten to. . . escape. Nobody entertained the thought that they would stand and fight a pitched battle. That was not the Indian way.'
Charles Neider, *The Great West,* 1958.

'The Indians were supplied with . . . the latest model of repeating rifles and ammunition. Their Winchester repeaters were far superior to our men's single-shot rifles.'
C. King, 5th Cavalry.

'Custer went in to die, and his fighting was superb.'
Yellow Horse.

'Never before had the Sioux people been so united . . . Never before had the Sioux warriors been so ably led.'
Stephen E. Amboise, Crazy Horse and Custer, *1975.*

Painting made in 1899 by E.S. Paxson, thought to be accurate.

Against Custer

'The honour of his country weighed lightly . . . against the glorious name of "Geo. A. Custer". The hardship and danger to his men were worthy of little consideration when . . . promotion floated before the excited mind of our Lieut.-Colonel.'
T. Ewert, 7th Cavalry.

'When Bloody Knife [a scout] reported back to Custer, he begged Custer to use extreme caution, declaring that there were more Sioux ahead than the soldiers had bullets . . . Custer brushed the warning aside.'
Stephen E. Amboise, Crazy Horse and Custer, *1975.*

'Custer advanced much more quickly than he had been ordered to do . . . he split his forces into three parts . . . The attack was one of the greatest fiascos of the US Army.'
People in the West, *Internet site, 1997.*

'General Terry sent a confidential report to the War Department placing the blame for the disaster upon Custer because he had disobeyed orders . . . [Elizabeth Custer] forgot her grief and began a long campaign to keep the name of the Boy General bright and shining in history.'
Dee Brown, The Westerners, *1974.*

However, finding out about this battle and Custer's role in it is very difficult:

- All US soldiers involved were killed.
- Indian accounts are conflicting.
- A myth grew up after the battle about Custer that has clouded people's views.

Use the information in Source 2 to judge Custer. The charge is: 'Custer led his men to their deaths because he only cared about glory for himself.' Innocent or guilty?

---

1. Why did the discovery of gold in the Black Hills in 1874 lead to war?

Using the information in this unit and any other information you have, write your own account of the Battle of the Little Bighorn.

---

2. What is your verdict on Custer? Give reasons to justify your decision.

What problems were there in reaching your verdict?

ATROCITIES

The history of the Plains Wars is filled with examples of atrocities. Traditionally, blame has been directed against Indians, but recently some writers have focused on white atrocities. The film *Soldier Blue* in 1970 (Source 1) showed the massacre at Sand Creek. The film shocked audiences with its graphic depiction of Indians being butchered by US soldiers. The truth is that both sides committed appalling atrocities that cannot be justified. This unit presents evidence to examine why this happened.

SOURCE 1

Soldier Blue, *1970.*

SOURCE 2

A) Women and children would mutilate the victim, cutting off parts, slicing through muscles, and the like, to make sure the dead warrior could not function again in the afterlife . . . Sometimes the severed genitals were stuffed into the victim's mouth to indicate Indian hatred for the victim.

Gerald F. Kreyche, Visions of the American West, *1989.*

B) Eyes torn out and laid on the rocks; noses cut off; ears cut off; chins hewn off . . . brains taken out and exposed; hands cut off; feet cut off; arms taken out of sockets.

Official Report on the massacre of troops from Fort Phil Kearny in 1866.

Source 3 shows a body mutilated by Indians. There are many accounts of atrocities carried out by US soldiers too. Source 4 is General Custer's justification for killing women and children at Washita in 1866 (see pages 80–81). The modern historian in Source 5 suggests reasons why officers might carry out atrocities.

SOURCE 3

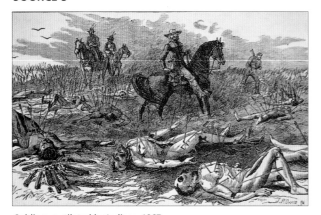

Soldiers mutilated by Indians, 1867.

SOURCE 4

In a struggle of this character it is impossible at all times to discriminate, particularly when, in a hand-to-hand conflict . . . the squaws are as dangerous as the warriors, while Indian boys . . . were found expert in the use of the pistol and bow and arrow.

SOURCE 5

Indian wars were used by ambitious officers as avenues for their own personal advancement . . . The army was at the centre of a vicious spiral of hatred, one level of fury escalating into a tier of bloodletting.

Robert V. Hine, The American West, *1984.*

Case Study: Sand Creek

About 600 Cheyenne, led by Black Kettle, had camped at Sand Creek. They were peaceful and had a US flag flying. Unfortunately for them Colonel John M. Chivington's Colorado volunteers attacked the village in November 1864 even though the Indians had hoisted a white flag. At least 105 women and children were killed, and about 28 warriors. Chivington later resigned his commission to avoid being punished, as the truth of the massacre became widely known.

SOURCE 6

Chivington had raised an infantry regiment . . . composed of all the riffraff on the frontier. Fortune seekers of every type, drunks, cardsharps, gunfighters, and all the Indian-haters of Denver signed up for a grand campaign. Their sole aim, and Chivington's, was to kill as many Indians as possible . . . and then get back to the warm comforts of the whorehouses and gambling dens in Denver.

Stephen E. Amboise, *Crazy Horse and Custer*, 1975.

SOURCE 7

Among the brilliant feats of arms in Indian warfare, the recent campaign of our Colorado volunteers will stand with few rivals . . . Colorado soldiers have again covered themselves with glory.

Rocky Mountain News, *1864.*

SOURCE 8

'I have heard that the whole Indian war had been brought on for selfish purposes. Colonel Chivington was running for Congress in Colorado . . . and that last spring he was looking for an order to go to the front . . . to carry out his electioneering purposes.'

Testimony of John S. Smith, *1864.*

SOURCE 9

'I did not see a body of man, woman, or child but was scalped, and in many instances their bodies were mutilated in the most horrible . . . these atrocities that were committed were with the knowledge of J. M. Chivington . . . I heard of numerous instances in which men had cut out the private parts of females and . . . wore them over their hats.'

Testimony of Lieutenant James Connor, *1864.*

SOURCE 10

'I believed the Indians in the camp were hostile to whites. That they were of the same tribes with those who had murdered many persons and destroyed much valuable property . . . I had no reason to believe that Black Kettle and the Indians with him were in good faith at peace with the whites.'

Testimony of Colonel J. M. Chivington, *1864.*

---

1. Why did Indians commit atrocities (Source 2)?
2. Use Sources 4 and 5 to explain why some army leaders committed atrocities.
3. What happened at Sand Creek?

---

4. Source 7 is untrue. Why was it printed?
5. What evidence is there that Chivington was lying?
6. Chivington had been a Methodist minister who had even stood out against the evils of slavery. How could such a Christian man have done this at Sand Creek?

GREAT PLAINS MASSACRE

The end of the buffalo herds

At one time it looked as if the buffalo would run forever. The introduction of the horse allowed Plains Indians to kill very large numbers of buffalo, but this still allowed millions to roam the Great Plains. During our period this was to change drastically, leading to their near extinction in North America: this was the 'Great Plains Massacre'. How could this dreadful situation have arisen?

There are several reasons why buffalo numbers declined:

- hunted by Plains Indians for their survival;
- white settlers drove the herds away;
- railroads drove the herds away;
- the stupidity of the buffalo made them sitting targets;
- white hunters killed vast numbers for their skins and tongues for money;
- it was fashionable for whites to shoot them and decorate their homes with them;
- it became Government policy to exterminate them.

The following sources illustrate some of these points.

SOURCE 1

Dickinson county has a buffalo hunter named Mr Warnock, who has killed as high as 658 in one winter . . . Ford county has twenty men who each have killed five times that number in one winter. The best on record, however, is that of Tom Dixon, who killed 120 at one stand in 40 minutes, and who from the 15th of September to the 20th of October, killed 2,173 buffalo.

Dodge City Times, 1877.

SOURCE 2

It seemed that the fine buggy tops, sledge bodies, book bindings, furniture and wall coverings – all the things that needed a strong, elastic leather, had been made from buffalo skins for years.

Mari Sandoz, The Buffalo Hunters, 1954.

SOURCE 4

[The hunters] have done more in the last two years, and will do more in the next year, to settle the vexed Indian question than the entire regular army has done in the last thirty years . . . Let them kill, skin and sell until the buffaloes are exterminated. Then your prairies can be

SOURCE 3

Shooting buffalo from a train. One bizarre discovery was that if buffalo were on the north side of the train they would continue grazing. If they were on the south side they stampeded and even threw themselves against the train!

covered with speckled cattle, and the festive cowboy, who follows the hunter as a second forerunner of an advanced civilisation.

General Sheridan. This policy was supported by the President.

SOURCE 5

Rather dim-witted, buffalo tend to congregate in groups. When hunters using long-range rifles would kill the group leader, the herd would mill around for a long time, unable to move from danger until a new leader was chosen. Hunters called this leaderless gathering a 'stand', and they would slaughter up to fifty of the indecisive beasts before they would flee.

Gerald F. Kreyche, Visions of the American West, 1989.

What were consequences of this? The following sources graphically show the horror of it.

SOURCE 6

Most of the meat shot by the buffalo hunters of 1867 was left to rot on the prairie to fatten the wolves, the buzzards and the long-tailed magpies. The juices soaked the earth and would darken the surrounding grass into lushness for many years. The bleaching bones were so thick that large reaches of the country would look white as from eternal frost.

Mari Sandoz, The Buffalo Hunters, 1954.

SOURCE 9

Photograph of buffalo skulls, 1880s.

SOURCE 7

1881 – 14,000 hides at $3.50

1882 – 35–40,000 hides at $3.50

1883 – 6–7,000 at a slight increase over last year

1884 – less than 2,500 hides, thought to be hold-overs from the previous year for a better market

1885 – little or no hides.

Joseph Ullman, Chicago Merchant.

---

1. a) Why did buffalo numbers decline?

  b) How many were there in: 1860; 1890; after 1900?

SOURCE 8

In Montana most of the hunters . . . in 1883 . . . found nothing but bones and very hungry swarms of buffalo gnats. They came back bankrupt and finally drifted into mining, cowboying, or followed the outlaw.

Mari Sandoz, The Buffalo Hunters, 1954.

The reality was that out of the estimated 60 million buffalo on the Great Plains in 1860, there were only 250 in 1890, before falling to less than 100 after 1900.

---

2. What were the causes of the extermination? Use Sources 1 to 4 to illustrate your answer.

3. Use Sources 6 to 9 to explain the consequences of this.

4. a) The extermination of the buffalo was Government policy to get rid of the Native American 'problem'. Can this policy be justified?

  b) What can we learn about Government attitudes towards the Indians from this?

IMPRISONMENT

We have already seen the creation of 'the Frontier', separating White USA from the Indian Territories. Helped by ideas such as Manifest Destiny, the Frontier moved steadily further West (see pages 60–61). This process got properly underway in 1830 when President Jackson passed the Removal Act designed to move Indians west of the Mississippi into 'Indian Territory'. The removals that followed were brutal, with many dying on the journey. This hostile writer sums it up (Source 1).

SOURCE 1

The rapid progress upon the continent will not permit the lands which are required for civilisation to be surrendered to savage tribes for hunting grounds. The government has always demanded the removal of the Indians when their lands were required for agricultural purposes by advancing settlements.

Secretary of the Interior, 1862.

SOURCE 2

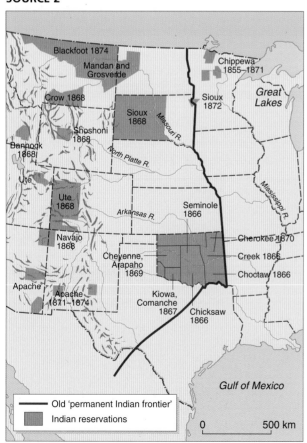

- Old 'permanent Indian frontier'
- ▨ Indian reservations

0   500 km

Reservations in 1875.

By the 1860s many Plains Indians had made two, three, or more removals to lands thought unwanted by any white settlers. As the numbers of settlers grew and available land for removals ran out, the Government turned to its reservation policy: we have seen that this was a major factor in the Plains Wars. Source 2 shows reservations in 1875. There were many justifications for this policy (Source 3).

SOURCE 3

The measures to which we are indebted for an improved condition of affairs are: the concentration of the Indians upon suitable reservations, and supplying them with the means for engaging in agricultural pursuits, and for their education and moral training.

Commissioner of Indian Affairs, 1869.

Reservations would turn Indians into 'Americans'. A great emphasis was placed on the education of the young: Indian children were forced to wear white American clothes, were taught white American beliefs, and were forced to speak in English. This was part of the process known as 'deculturisation'.

This led to the Dawes or Allotment Act (Source 4) designed to destroy Indian tribal culture by allocating land to individual family groups.

SOURCE 4

A) Allot the lands in the reservations individually to any Indian located there in quantities as follows:

To each head of a family, one-quarter of a section;

To each single person over eighteen years of age, one-eighth of a section;

To each orphan child under eighteen years of age, one-eighth of a section;

To each other single person under eighteen years . . . one-sixteenth of a section.

Dawes Act, 1887. (One section = 640 acres.)

B) It establishes a policy which would help the Indians to become independent farmers by making them individual land-holders. This looks to the gradual breaking up of the reservations on which the Indians are shut from all wholesome contact with our civilisation. This loosens the fatal tribal bonds by bringing the Indians under our laws, and making the way for their entrance into citizenship.

Indian Rights Association on the Dawes Act, 1887.

It is no surprise that the Dawes Act left a huge surplus of Indian lands ready to be sold to white settlers! Reservations became appalling places (Source 5).

SOURCE 5

By the late 1880s reservations had become virtual concentration camps. Most were on barren lands useless for farming and devoid of game. Providing subsidies and food for over 200,000 Indian people was big business. The distribution system quickly became a corrupt network of government agents and their partners known as the Indian Ring. Robbing nations of their meagre government subsidies, the Indian Ring left the people in abject poverty.

500 Nations, *Microsoft CD-Rom, 1995.*

SOURCE 6

Indians on a reservation, 1880s. Note the government issue tent and metal utensils.

SOURCE 7

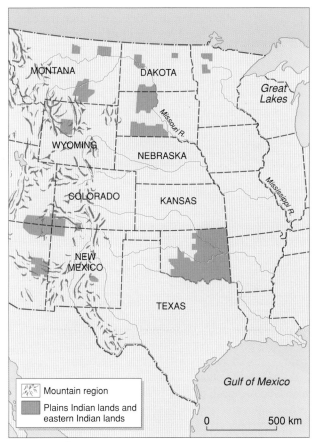

Reservations by 1900.

Source 6 shows a bleak reservation scene. Indians were encouraged to become lazy and rely on their meagre handouts; and there was an inadequate attempt to teach them farming methods. They took little pride in their surroundings, as they often had to move on. An historian explains: 'Reservations were a good thing only as long as they did not contain land desired by the whites.' Alcoholism, despair, and even suicide became problems. The scale of the removal and reservation policies can be seen in Source 7 showing the tiny amount of Indian land left by the end of the century.

1. a) What was the Removal Act?
   b) What was the situation by the 1860s?
2. What was the intention of the reservation system?
3. a) What did the Dawes Act do?
   b) What were the real intentions of the Act?
4. Use Sources 5 and 6 to describe conditions.
5. What do Sources 2 and 7 tell us about Indian lands?

6. a) Why did the Government pass the Removal and Reservation Acts?
   b) What were the consequences of these?
7. Do the consequences of this prove the Government wanted to destroy the Indians?

'BURY MY HEART AT WOUNDED KNEE'

Phase 4 : 1877–90

The victory at Little Bighorn in 1876 was very shallow for the Indians. Their very success ensured their downfall as a shocked white nation mustered its full resources to defeat them. Indians were rounded up and put on reservations, or forced to flee in temporary hope of escaping the inevitable. The imprisonment and deaths of Indian leaders such as Crazy Horse only increased their desperation. In such a state people cling to any hope: in the case of the Plains Indians this was the Ghost Dance (Source 1), prophesised by a medicine man called Wovoka.

SOURCE 2

The second coming – an Indian Messiah – was advancing through the West. If the Indian peoples refrained from all violence, if they were virtuous and honest, and if they danced the Ghost Dance, they would hasten the coming of the new world. Then all the whites would disappear. All the dead ancestors would come back to life (and) the buffalo would return . . .

Joining hands, the dancers shuffled sidewards in great concentric circles. The intensity of the dance increased as they sang and prayed themselves into a delirium, singing of the world to come. Exhaustion brought on rapturous visions.

'The Wild West', Channel 4 TV, 1995.

Dancers wore ghost shirts to protect them from white men's bullets, and they often cut themselves. From October 1890, the miserable sight of thousands of Ghost Dancers terrified the US authorities into action: they invaded reservations to force Indians to stop the dance. One of the casualties was Sitting Bull who was wrongly believed to be behind the Ghost Dance. His murder during a bungled arrest in December 1890 made the situation more tense as thousands of Indians fled in terror.

The final act was played out on 29 December when Colonel James W. Forsyth led over 400 men of the 7th Cavalry into the camp of Big Foot who had surrendered. In a tense encounter a shot was fired that led to a carnage still causing bitterness today. Sources 3 and 4 are two conflicting interpretations.

SOURCE 3

Big Foot, flying the flag of truce within his encampment, was dying from pneumonia. His people were dying from fear of the white soldiers who had come to take revenge for the defeat of their unit, the 7th Cavalry, at Little Bighorn . . . in 1876. All the soldiers needed was the smallest excuse to begin the massacre.

A single shot . . . was fired from the soldiers . . . When the rain of ammunition ceased, over 300 Lakota people lay dead . . . The dead were Lakota men who had been disarmed before the weapons fire began, women, many with babes in arms or waiting to be born, and children.

Wounded Knee Internet Site, 1997.

SOURCE 1

Ghost Dancers, Arapaho tribe, Oklahoma Reservation, 1891.

SOURCE 4

There is nothing to conceal or apologise for in the Wounded Knee Battle – beyond the killing of a wounded buck by a hysterical recruit. The firing was begun by the Indians and continued until they stopped – with the one exception noted above . . . The Indians at Wounded Knee brought their own destruction as surely as any people ever did. Their attack on the troops was as treacherous as any in the history of Indian warfare.

General E. D. Scott, Official Investigation of Wounded Knee.

The reality is probably closer to this view by a prominent historian (Source 5).

SOURCE 5

The vast majority of both Indians and soldiers were . . . decent, ordinary people. They suddenly found themselves thrust into battle. It is time that Wounded Knee be viewed for what it was – a regrettable, tragic accident of war that neither side intended.

Robert M. Utley, The Last Days of the Sioux Nation, *1963.*

SOURCE 6

The aftermath of the massacre at Wounded Knee.

Source 6 shows the scene after the massacre. Wounded Knee represented not only the end of the Indian Wars; it represented the end of a way of life. As Black Elk said, 'I can see that something else died there in the bloody mud, and was buried in the blizzard. A people's dream died there. It was a beautiful dream.'

---

1. What happened to the Plains Indians after 1876?
2. a) Use Sources 1 and 2 to explain what the Ghost Dance was.

   b) How did the US army respond to this?
3. Use the text and Sources 3 to 6 to explain what probably happened at Wounded Knee.

4. a) Why is it usually more reliable to study the views of modern historians (Source 5), than primary sources, or modern one-sided ones (Sources 3 and 4)?

   b) How can historians use sources that are known to be unreliable?
5. The Wounded Knee Internet site presents the Indian perspective of what happened, and an attempt to get official condemnation of the Army's actions. It invites visitors to sign petitions about related issues and the treatment of modern Native Americans. What does this tell us about modern Native American feelings?

END OF AN ERA

Source 1 invites you to have a taste of the Wild West in comfort for the price of a ticket. In 1883 former scout and hero of the dime novel 'Buffalo Bill' Cody started the first Wild West show. Many others followed and played to delighted audiences into the 1930s. The Wild West was being turned into a myth: Hollywood would complete this transformation.

Early in the century the Government had considered that it would take 500 years to complete the white population of the West. In reality, the pace of occupation and change had been at breakneck speed. The permanent Frontier we saw in 1840 had not only moved further west – it had now gone. With this came the birth of the modern USA as this professor recognised in a speech in 1893:

SOURCE 1

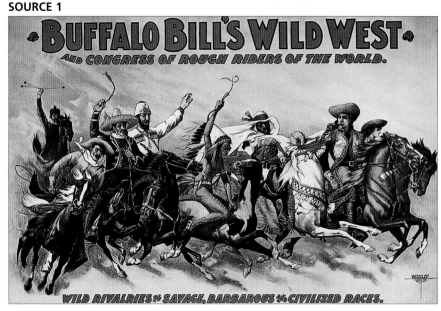

Poster for Buffalo Bill's Wild West show, 1898.

SOURCE 2

This expansion westward with its new opportunities, its continuous touch with the simplicity of primitive society, provide the forces dominating American character. Four centuries from the discovery of America, at the end of a hundred years of life under the Constitution, the frontier has gone, and with its going has closed the first period of American history.

Frederick Jackson Turner.

SOURCE 3

	Whites	Indians
1890	46,000,000	122,000
1900	56,500,00	117,000
1950	124,781,000	165,000

Even within the period, the processes of change, development, and technology were so rapid that some institutions were now things of the past: trailblazers; buffalo hunters; pony express riders; open ranges; cavalry soldiers and their forts. The Plains Indians were now imprisoned within reservations that were to contribute to serious social problems in the 20th century. However, the demise of the Indians was necessary for the new west to develop: Source 3 shows how extensive this was.

As this phase in the USA's development ended so another one began: the emergence of the USA in the 20th century as the world's most powerful country. Would this have been possible without the development of the American West?

1. Look at the diagram on page 35. Make your own version of this with the title 'The American West'. Work out the main areas and what material to include in each.

2. Use the evidence from question 1 to copy out and fill in these tables:

The American West

Good features	Bad features

Main changes	Effects/consequences

3. 'The demise of the Indians was necessary for the new West to develop.' Can this be justified?

4. Was the West really 'wild'?

INDEX

IMPRINTS AND ACKNOWLEDGEMENTS

Published by Collins Educational
An imprint of HarperCollins *Publishers* Ltd
77–85 Fulham Palace Road
Hammersmith
London W6 8JB

© HarperCollins *Publishers* Ltd 1998
First published 1998

ISBN 0 00 327112 9

James Green asserts the moral right to be identified as the author of this work.

British Library Cataloguing in Publication Data
A catalogue record for this book is available from the British Library.

Edited by Lorimer Poultney and Steve Attmore
Design by Claire Brodmann
Cover design by Derek Lee
Map artwork by Jeff Edwards
Illustrations by James Green (pages 4, 16, 22, 29, 32, 35, 39, 42, 52, 60, 62, 67, 78)
Illustration by Robert Calow, Eikon Ltd (page 23)
Picture research by Celia Dearing
Production by Sue Cashin
Printed and bound by Printing Express Ltd., Hong Kong.

ACKNOWLEDGEMENTS

Every effort has been made to contact the holders of copyright material, but if any have been inadvertently overlooked the publishers will be pleased to make the necessary arrangements at the first opportunity.

Copyright © from *Visions of the American West*, by Gerald F. Kreyche. Reprinted with permission of The University Press of Kentucky; Reed Consumer Books ltd for two extracts from *Cowboys* by Royal B Hassrick, published in 1974 by Octopus Books; *Manifest Destiny* by Frederick Merk © Alfred A. Knopf Incorporated; extract from *Westering Women* by Sandra Myers, courtesy of University of New Mexico Press 1982.

The publishers would like to thank the following for permission to reproduce photographs (T = Top, B = Bottom, L = Left, R = Right).

© Amon Carter Museum, Fort Worth, Texas, 1961.205 'Smoke of a .45' Charles M. Russell, oil on canvas, 1908 page 64; National Museum of American Art, Washington DC/Art Resource, NY pages 9T, 9B, 11T 46, 54; Bridgeman Art Library, London/Private Collection pages 44, 55 /New York Historical Society 63T /D F Barry, Bismarck, Dakota 82; © Courtesy Museum of Art, Brigham Young University. All rights reserved, 'Saints Driven from Jackson County Missouri' by C C A Christensen page 56; California Historical Society, gift of Mr and Mrs Reginald Walker 'Cattle Drive #1' circa 1877 by James Walker page 30; Courtesy Colorado Historical Society (Neg. no. F28537) page 53; Corbis-Bettmann pages 34T, 93 /UPI 42L; Denver Public Library, Western History Department page 59; Courtesy of the Burton Historical Collection of the Detroit Public Library page 89; Mary Evans Picture Library pages 57, 83 /ILN 21; Courtesy Ronald Grant Archive/Warner Brothers page 3B, /Guild 11B 'United International Pictures 5T /MGM 73; The Hutchison Library/Jon Burbank page 7TR/John Dowman 7BL /Andrew Hill 7TL /Sabina Pusch 7BR; Idaho State Historical Society page 19T; Kansas State Historical Society pages 33, 42R; Courtesy The Kobal Collection/Orion page 12 /Avco Embassy 86; Nebraska State Historical Society/Solomon D Butcher Collection pages 43BL, 47T, 47B, 49; Rare Books Division, The New York Public Library, Astor, Lenox and Tilden Foundations page 50; Peter Newark's Western Americana pages 3T, 5B, 8, 10, 13, 15, 17, 19B, 20, 24, 25, 27B, 28, 29, 34N, 40, 41, 43BR, 51, 58, 61, 63B, 66, 68, 71L, 72, 74–77, 81, 85, 86B, 88, 91, 94; Smithsonian Institution photo 3237a page 80, photo 81-9626 page 92; Used by permission Utah State Historical Society, all rights reserved page 27T; West Point Museum Collections, US Military Academy page 48; State Historical Society of Wisconsin page 43T; Wyoming Division of Cultural Resources page 69; Beinecke Rare Book and Manuscript Library, Yale University page 71R.

Cover photograph: Bridgeman Art Library/Private Collection, 'A Dash for the Timber' by Frederick Remington.